United States Army

Letter From the Secretary of War

Transmitting Letter of the Chief Signal Officer on the Climate of Oregon...

United States Army

Letter From the Secretary of War
Transmitting Letter of the Chief Signal Officer on the Climate of Oregon...

ISBN/EAN: 9783337013752

Printed in Europe, USA, Canada, Australia, Japan

Cover: Foto ©ninafisch / pixelio.de

More available books at **www.hansebooks.com**

50TH CONGRESS, }
1st Session. }

SENATE.

{ EX. DOC.
{ No. 282.

LETTER

FROM

THE SECRETARY OF WAR,

TRANSMITTING

LETTER OF THE CHIEF SIGNAL OFFICER

ON THE

CLIMATE OF OREGON AND WASHINGTON TERRITORY.

OCTOBER 20, 1888.—Referred to the Committee on Agriculture and Forestry
and ordered to be printed.

WASHINGTON:
GOVERNMENT PRINTING OFFICE.
1889.

LETTER

THE SECRETARY OF WAR,

TRANSMITTING

Letter of the Chief Signal Officer on the climate of Oregon and Washington Territory.

OCTOBER 20, 1888. – Referred to the Committee on Agriculture and Forestry and ordered to be printed.

LETTER OF TRANSMITTAL.

WAR DEPARTMENT,
Washington City, October 19, 1888.

The Secretary of War has the honor to transmit to the United States Senate a report, dated the 17th instant, from the Chief Signal Officer of the Army, together with charts and tables prepared under his direction, upon the climate of Oregon, and upon the climatic and other conditions of the agricultural districts of eastern Oregon and Washington Territory, and also upon such other matters as relate thereto, the same being furnished in response to Senate resolution of July 26, 1888.

WILLIAM C. ENDICOTT,
Secretary of War.

The PRESIDENT PRO TEMPORE UNITED STATES SENATE.

3

THE CLIMATE OF OREGON AND WASHINGTON TERRITORY.

SIGNAL OFFICE, WAR DEPARTMENT,
Washington City, October 17, 1888.

SIR: I have the honor to herewith transmit charts and tables on subject-matter relating to the climate of Oregon and Washington Territory, as called for by the following resolution of the Senate of the United States:

IN THE SENATE OF THE UNITED STATES, JULY 26, 1888.

Resolved, That the Secretary of War be, and is hereby, directed to transmit to the Senate the reports that have been prepared, under the direction of the Chief Signal Officer of the Army, upon the climate of Oregon, and upon the climatic and other conditions of the agricultural districts of eastern Oregon and Washington Territory, together with such tables and other matters as relate thereto, with such additions, corrections, and alterations as may be deemed advisable by the Chief Signal Officer.

Attest:

ANSON G. MCCOOK, *Secretary.*

The following list shows the charts and tables accompanying this report, which, in all cases, cover Oregon and Washington Territory:

Appendix No. 1. List and location of stations in Oregon and one in Idaho, with length of record for which precipitation data are given, together with monthly and annual means at twenty-eight stations, for an average period of nine years.

Appendix No. 2. List and location of stations in Washington Territory and one in Montana, with length of record for which precipitation data are given, together with monthly and annual means at thirty-one stations, for an average period of seven years.

Appendix No. 3. Percentages of mean monthly rain-fall at seventeen stations in Washington Territory, twenty stations in Oregon, and one each in Idaho and Montana.

Appendix No. 4. List and location of stations in Oregon and one in Idaho, with length of record for which temperature data are given, together with monthly and annual means at thirty stations, for an average period of seven years.

Appendix No. 5. List and location of stations in Washington Territory and one in Montana, with length of record for which temperature data are given, together with monthly and annual means at twenty-eight stations, for an average period of eight years.

Appendix No. 6. Variability of temperature in Oregon and Washington Territory from October to March, for twelve stations in Oregon, ten in Washington Territory, and one each in Idaho and Montana.

Chart No. 1. Mean annual precipitation.

Chart No. 2. Mean precipitation for the wet season, from October to April, inclusive.

Chart No. 3. Mean precipitation for the dry season, from May to September, inclusive.

Chart No. 4. Average number of rainy days, from October to March, inclusive.

Chart No. 5. Mean annual temperature.

Chart No. 6. Mean summer temperature.

Chart No. 7. Mean winter temperature.

Chart No. 8. One index-map (which will serve as a base-map), showing location of stations in Oregon and Washington Territory.

PRECIPITATION.

On Chart No. 1 is shown the mean annual rain-fall of Oregon and Washington Territory. Although the rain-fall along the immediate coast of the Pacific Ocean, ranging from 70 to over 107 inches, is the heaviest in the United States, yet, contrary to the generally-received opinion, this enormous rain-fall does not cover the entire area of these States, but only 6 per centum of them. On the other hand, it has been represented that the interior portions of Oregon and Washington Territory were almost rainless. The fallacy of this statement is shown by Chart No. 1, whereby it appears that the smallest recorded rain-fall, at Pleasant Grove, for two years and four months,

5

is over 9.5 inches. The area over which less than 10 inches of rain falls does not cover 5 per
centum of either State, and by a curious coincidence it appears, by the report of Second Lieutenant
Frank Greene, Signal Corps, on the Interior Wheat Lands of Oregon and Washington Territory,
that over the greater part of this region of small rain-fall wheat is grown without irrigation.
Indeed, according to Lieutenant Greene's report, crops can be grown in nine-tenths of both these
States without irrigation, and in the other tenth it is probable that on this point the character of
the soil has as important a bearing as deficient rain-fall. An examination of Charts 2 and 3, of
the mean seasonal rain-fall for the wet season, from October to April, and the dry season, from May
to September, discloses that in the eastern half of these States the rain-fall during the dry season
is about half what it is during the wet season. It follows from this equable distribution of rain-fall
throughout the year, that agricultural operations are more fruitful with a small rain-fall than in
some sections of other States with considerably larger precipitation. The idea is also prevalent
that during the wet season the rain is continuous. Chart No. 4, showing the average number of
rainy days in Oregon and Washington Territory from October to March, inclusive, exhibits the
exact condition of affairs. Along the coast and adjacent sections of Oregon and Washington
Territory, where rainy days are most frequent, it will be observed that every other day in October
and March is without rain, while in intervening months the frequency of rain is somewhat greater,
rising in December to three days out of four. In middle and eastern Oregon, however, the rain
falls with lesser frequency, according to its distance from the coast, nowhere oftener, on the average, than every other day in Washington Territory, and about once in three days in Oregon during December, the rainy month; while during October and March the weather is usually clear and
fine, rain falling over the greater part of these sections only one day in five or six.

An examination of the percentages of rain-fall for the different months has also been made (see
Appendix No. 3). If the rain fell equally throughout the year it would follow that 8.3 per cent.
should fall each month. For the sake of comparative purposes, it has been assumed that a *wet*
month is one where 12.7 per cent. of rain falls, and a *very wet* month where double the usual amount
falls, or 17 per cent. In like manner, a *dry* month is one where only 4 per cent. of the annual rain-
fall occurs; and a *very dry* one where 2 per cent. or less, is noted.

It appears from the record that there are many places in Oregon and Washington Territory
where there is no *very wet* month, but at exceptional stations with a *very wet* month, such excess
of rain fall occurs in December or January, with percentages of the annual rain-fall rarely exceed-
ing 18 or 19. During the remaining months of the year, except July and August, it is a tolerably
general rule that the rain-fall is fairly distributed, with a greater tendency to heavier rains in
February and November than in May, June, September, and October. Nearly all of Oregon and
Washington Territory experiences very dry Julys and Augusts; the rain-fall, fortunately for these
States, being deficient, while clear and sunshiny days are particularly frequent at that season of
the year when the staple crops have fully ripened. The alternation of wet and dry seasons renders
it possible for crops to be raised, with certainty that the rain-fall will come during certain months,
and be followed later by fair weather suitable for harvesting.

TEMPERATURE.

On Chart No. 5 is represented the mean annual temperature. It shows at a glance the remarkably equable temperature conditions which prevail in these States, the entire range of mean annual
temperature over this territory being but 8.5°, from 45.3° at Fort Colville, in northeastern Washington Ter. to 53.8° at Ashland, Oregon. The mean annual temperature, however, is not always
a satisfactory evidence of equable temperature throughout the year, but an examination of Chart
No. 6 shows the mildness of the mean summer temperature from June to August. In both States
there is but a small area, the valley of the Upper Columbia, where the mean temperature rises
above 70° Fahrenheit, for the summer months; at the same time the temperature in the neighbor-
hood of Puget Sound and along the coast region is remarkably equable and comfortable, and in
300 miles of latitude the entire range is practically insignificant, being only 3.6° Fahrenheit, ranging
from 55.7° at Port Angeles, Wash., to 59.3° at Fort Stevens, Oregon. During the winter
months, December, January, and February, the mean temperature (see Chart No. 7) of more than

one-half of these States is above the freezing-point, and along the immediate Gulf coast ranges between 40° and 45°. The only portions of Oregon and Washington Territory in which freezing temperatures prevail for any considerable time, are, in the more elevated regions including, in Washington Territory, the great plains of the Columbia River, and in southeastern Oregon the high plateaus near the headwaters of the tributaries of the Columbia and Snake Rivers.

With a view to determining, in the most exact way, the equability of temperature in Oregon and Washington Territory, the temperature variability of a large number of stations has been computed from October to March (see Appendix No. 6), these months being selected as those in which the greatest changes are experienced.

The *variability* of temperature means the change which takes place in the daily mean temperature from one day to another, irrespective of whether the temperature rises or falls, and is the surest test of equability and freedom from violent changes.

It appears that the variability during these months in Oregon and Washington Territory rarely exceeds one and a half degrees Fahrenheit, and in many cases is less than one degree; thus showing in these States an equability of temperature which is unequaled in any other part of the United States, except along the immediate coast line in California, from Cape Mendocino to San Diego.

To summarize, Oregon and Washington Territory are favored with a climate of unusual mildness and equability; while the immediate coast regions have very heavy rain falls, yet such rain occurs during the winter months of December to February, and in all cases the wet season gives place gradually to the dry season, during July and August. While the preponderating amount of rain falls during the winter, yet the spring, early summer, and late fall are marked by moderate rains at not infrequent intervals.

These climatic conditions favor to a marked extent the growth of most cereals and other important staple crops.

As to the constituents of the soil and the distribution of arable land, this office is not in possession of the necessary data on which to express a satisfactory opinion.

I am, very respectfully, your obedient servant,

A. W. GREELY,
Chief Signal Officer.

The SECRETARY OF WAR.

APPENDIX No. 1.

Precipitation data for Oregon.

Name of station.	County.	Latitude.	Longitude.	Elevation.	Record. Length. (Yrs. Mos.)	Record. From—	Record. To (inclusive)—	Remarks as to observers and character of records.
		° ′	° ′	Feet.	Yrs. Mos.			
Albany (near)	Linn	44 35	122 50	600	19 6	Jan., 1866	Dec., 1887	Jan., 1866, to Jan., 1868, inclusive, S. M. W. Hindman. Jan., 1870, to Dec., 1887, John Briggs.
Ashland	Jackson	42 12	122 28	1,940	4 0	Jan., 1884	Dec., 1887	Jan., 1884, from "Resources of Oregon." Feb., 1884, to Dec., 1887, Signal Service.
Astoria	Clatsop	46 11	123 48	50	28 9	Aug., 1850	May, 1888	Aug., 1850, to Sept., 1851, United States post hospital. Sept., 1853, to Dec., 1876, L. Wilson, U. S. Coast Survey. Dec., 1883, to May, 1888, Signal Service.
Bandon	Coos	43 05	124 15		10 0	Jan., 1878	Dec., 1887	George Bennett.
Blockhouse	Benton	44 25	123 30		4 2	Mar., 1858	Dec., 1862	United States post hospital.
Dalles, Fort	Columbia	45 33	120 50	350	13 0	July, 1850	Mar., 1856	Do.
East Portland	Multnomah	45 30	122 35		4 0	Jan., 1884	Dec., 1887	George Wigg, M. D.
Empire City	Coos	43 22	124 10		5 10			
Eola	Polk	44 57	123 54	500	18 0	Jan., 1870	Dec., 1887	T. Pearce.
Harney, Camp	Grant	43 00	119 00		11 8	Dec., 1867	May, 1880	United States post hospital.
Hoskins, Fort	Polk	45 06	120 26		7 9	Dec., 1856	Sept., 1864	Do.
Klamath, Fort	Klamath	42 40	121 50	4,200	15 8	Nov., 1861	Dec., 1887	Nov., 1861, to Dec., 1882, United States post hospital. Jan., 1883, to Dec., 1887, Signal Service.
La Grande	Union	45 22	118 18		1 7	June 1886	Dec., 1887	J. K. Romig.
Lakeview	Lake	49 12	120 12	5,096	4 2	Nov., 1883	Dec., 1887	Signal Service, except Jan., 1884, from "Resources of Oregon."
Linkville	Klamath	42 15	121 45	4,250	4 0	Jan., 1884	Dec., 1887	Signal Service.
Mount Angel	Marion	45 05	122 50		1 7	June, 1886	Dec., 1887	F. Barnabas Held.
Oregon City	Clackamas	45 20	4 22 16	200	3 0	Jan., 1854	Mar., 1850	Rev. G. H. Atkinson.
Portland	Multnomah	45 30	122 36	*150 /80	19 10	Apr., 1858	Dec., 1887	Apr., 1858, to Aug., 1850, G. H. Stebbins. Jan., 1870, to Oct., 1871, R. W. Gilliland and J. S. Read. Nov., 1871, to Dec., 1887, Signal Service.
Port Orford	Curry	42 44	124 29	50	2 10	June, 1852	July, 1850	United States post hospital.
Roseburgh	Douglas	43 10	123 20	523	10 8	July, 1877	Dec., 1887	Signal Service.
Stevens, Fort	Clatsop	46 12	123 57		15 1	Nov., 1865	Feb., 1883	United States post hospital.
The Dalles	Wasco	45 30	121 12	116	13 0	Jan., 1875	Dec., 1887	Samuel L. Brooks.
Umatilla	Umatilla	45 55	119 22		5 8	Aug., 1877	Mar., 1883	Signal Service.
Umpqua, Fort	Douglas	43 42	124 10	8	5 10	Aug., 1856	May, 1862	United States post hospital.
Warner, Camp	Lake	42 28	119 42		5 3	Aug., 1869	July, 1874	Do.
Watson, Camp	Grant	44 22	119 48		1 9	June, 1867	Mar., 1869	Do.
Yamhill, Fort	Yamhill	45 21	122 15		9 0	Nov., 1856	Apr., 1866	Do.
Boisé City, Idaho	Ada	43 37	116 8	2,790	10 5	July, 1877	May, 1888	Signal Service.

* Stebbins.   † Signal Service.

Statement showing the precipitation in inches and hundredths.

ALBANY (near), OREGON.

Year.	Jan.	Feb.	Mar.	Apr.	May.	June	July.	Aug.	Sept.	Oct.	Nov.	Dec.	Annual.
1866	14.15	4.60	11.71	1.89	5.33	......	0.01	0.75	......	2.80	4.88	8.22	158.70
1867	14.45	10.71	2.96	5.20	2.45	......	0.36	......	2.10				......
1868	8.06	......	......	......	......	......	......	......	......	......	......	......	......
1878	*6.02	*8.00	*0.71	3.54	5.70	0.27	0.72	1.52	2.62	2.46	5.80	7.19	50.95
1880	11.19	5.31	3.61	2.62	3.21	1.18	0.85	0.68	1.11	1.12	1.76	9.47	41.86
1881	11.71	13.08	3.53	3.13	1.34	2.56	1.89	1.62	2.24	7.60	4.64	6.78	58.04
1882	2.22	10.07	3.47	4.32	1.28	0.41	0.81	0.04	0.41	7.07	4.15	11.04	48.00
1883	7.46	1.36	4.31	6.58	2.05	0.22	0.00	0.06	1.07	4.06	4.56	6.72	38.41
1884	3.91	8.00	3.12	6.30	0.89	3.33	1.87	0.43	5.61	2.85	2.18	7.83	45.23
1885	4.29	5.82	0.81	1.38	3.92	1.95	0.90	0.00	2.13	1.75	6.49	7.04	37.41
1886	9.92	3.34	3.19	2.06	1.79	8.96	0.79	T.	1.20	3.28	1.75	10.31	90.06
1887	12.58	4.30	0.03	4.55	2.91	1.21	0.00	0.09	1.67	0.97	5.99	14.21	57.64
Means	8.73	6.88	4.72	3.66	2.81	1.28	0.57	6.52	2.02	3.34	4.40	8.06	47.91

ASHLAND, OREGON.

Year.	Jan.	Feb.	Mar.	Apr.	May.	June	July.	Aug.	Sept.	Oct.	Nov.	Dec.	Annual.
1864	1.35	0.05	3.14	1.33	0.76	0.24	0.27	0.00	2.28	1.54	0.07	5.07	18.00
1865	2.44	4.55	0.01	1.52	3.74	2.40	0.02	0.00	1.18	1.58	8.02	3.32	24.73
1866	4.64	1.63	1.43	2.03	1.10	0.72	1.99	0.00	0.00	1.65	1.98	4.66	21.32
1867	4.96	2.71	0.06	3.39	1.15	0.74	0.33	0.04	0.66	0.58	0.94	3.38	19.87
Means	3.35	2.46	1.39	2.22	1.71	1.02	0.58	0.01	1.03	1.34	2.59	4.33	21.97

ASTORIA, OREGON.

Year.	Jan.	Feb.	Mar.	Apr.	May.	June	July.	Aug.	Sept.	Oct.	Nov.	Dec.	Annual.
1850	27.00(*)	16.05	6.10	4.36	6.05	2.85	0.00	0.06	1.80	6.70	13.20(*)	8.20	......
1851								2.30	1.91		13.26	7.90	186.35
1852									4.00		13.26	7.90	......
1853	5.00	5.15	......	9.32	2.17	5.23	0.03	3.08	0.62	4.57	4.06	10.18	160.35
1854	21.52	6.38	7.58	6.77	4.98	1.43	0.04	0.29	4.95	5.29	10.19	10.92	79.20
1855	5.68	3.28	3.84	6.42	3.98	8.12	3.00	0.38	1.84	6.91	7.33	10.74	59.17
1856	16.07	13.05	11.03	0.80	2.04	2.47	0.42	0.28	1.90	2.58	5.94	22.78	79.82
1857	8.58	6.00	6.83	5.28	2.40	1.26	2.30	3.40	3.12	4.88	8.06	12.44	88.36
1858	10.82	12.02	21.32	2.65	3.47	2.10	6.51	1.32	6.45	5.46	7.97	6.10	62.15
1859	13.54	6.05	5.88	5.69	5.04	1.40	1.35	0.78	2.54	7.02	12.44	6.90	70.65
1860	9.70	13.74	7.68	7.92	6.07	6.11	0.19	1.82	2.81	5.99	15.26	16.19	95.99
1861	7.60	5.17	17.41	4.09	2.55	1.36	2.16	1.50	2.31	3.23	3.44	10.98	81.32
1862	18.98	15.53	6.78	4.05	3.64	2.77	2.16	0.50	8.49	6.35	8.12	16.75	94.13
1863	11.64	7.52	13.05	8.12	1.23	3.85	0.87	0.45	4.79	2.16	12.16	14.27	75.70
1864	12.13	6.62	13.25	4.90	3.17	2.68	1.19	2.03	7.61	2.21	16.20	13.21	85.22
1865	16.16	7.39	11.83	7.31	4.52	5.74	0.94	2.17	1.34	0.93	17.72	15.50	100.40
1866	17.52	14.13	2.56	5.70	1.26	1.87	4.37	0.18	1.91	8.21	8.91	24.73	91.25
1867	3.56	4.94	9.06	6.08	4.59	2.76	0.62	0.02	0.33	3.52	8.25	14.08	57.74
1868	11.78	3.16	5.13	6.01	1.33	0.06	0.30	5.87	5.90	1.32	10.13	9.61	66.61
1869	14.89	6.90	8.98	5.82	3.47	3.73	0.73	1.96	2.70	1.81	10.31	10.11	71.19
1870	22.16	10.88	17.11	4.17	8.91	1.03	1.36	0.61	2.88	3.85	14.08	15.90	100.42
1871	8.26	17.37	9.50	7.62	2.54	2.11	0.97	0.61	1.34	4.77	7.10	11.32	73.70
1872	16.06	9.20	12.55	6.48	1.79	4.77	0.95	2.18	0.73	3.43	4.90	7.56	74.41
1873	17.86	12.69	6.99	5.67	3.73	5.06	0.98	2.21	3.90	1.53	13.01	7.82	80.89
1874	8.58	4.40	16.56	4.85	6.83	2.38	0.26	1.16	1.32	13.38	16.70	19.49	95.73
1875	11.91	12.19	12.55	8.70	6.29	4.63	3.55	1.78	1.65	*6.50	*12.00	*3.00	84.75
1876	8.73	7.13	2.56	4.59	1.36	2.04	1.39	1.63	6.22	6.40	2.63	6.55	49.38
1884	6.78	10.50	1.51	1.03	3.43	2.78	0.04	0.02	4.24	3.44	12.45	9.85	56.16
1885	13.34	5.60	7.23	4.99	3.85	2.03	2.58	0.56	4.39	5.87	4.84	16.86	71.59
1886	18.24	6.51	16.11	5.83	7.83	0.63	0.72	0.49	4.82	3.66	8.11	16.64	92.00
1888	13.84	4.12	6.64	4.04	0.70								......
Means	12.97	8.60	9.91	5.26	3.67	2.86	1.28	1.37	3.33	4.95	10.28	12.30	76.65

BANDON, OREGON.

Year.	Jan.	Feb.	Mar.	Apr.	May.	June	July.	Aug.	Sept.	Oct.	Nov.	Dec.	Annual.
1878	14.59	14.20	16.50	2.30	3.29	0.96	1.90	1.15	2.25	4.64	6.94	4.88	67.04
1879	10.10	10.88	15.60	3.78	7.79	1.30	1.29	2.18	2.97	6.22	7.73	12.47	81.79
1880	18.65	6.50	8.33	8.66	3.49	2.60	0.34	0.68	0.66	1.16	0.79	13.95	65.97
1881	14.21	17.82	4.31	1.34	1.79	0.11	0.91	0.68	2.51	7.13	5.32	11.80	73.94
1882	8.41	10.18	2.50	6.87	4.90	0.14	0.16	0.20	1.06	6.98	4.10	14.10	66.27
1883	8.97	3.54	4.08	9.34	2.83	0.32	*0.01	*0.27	5.59	3.90	7.83	48.33	
1884	4.00	8.72	5.20	3.96	9.42	1.22	1.05	0.00	5.12	3.12	3.93	13.95	52.09
1885	6.73	12.42	0.63	0.97	2.10	1.78	*0.09	0.22	2.22	2.45	18.21	13.27	60.83
1886	13.72	5.05	5.68	4.65	1.00	0.51	1.29	0.19	0.49	5.87	2.27	11.97	54.42
1887	16.29	6.17	7.07	6.47	5.11	0.47	6.15	0.05	1.15	1.43	8.87	14.54	84.46
Means	11.63	9.59	6.54	4.92	3.26	1.38	0.76	0.52	2.11	4.45	5.91	13.85	62.91

* Interpolated.　　| Incomplete, Schott.　　T. trace of precipitation.

S. Ex. 282———2

*Statement showing the precipitation in inches and hundredths—*Continued.

BLOCK HOUSE, OREGON.

Year.	Jan.	Feb.	Mar.	Apr.	May.	June.	July.	Aug.	Sept.	Oct.	Nov.	Dec.	Annual.
1858			9.55	7.29	5.46	2.57	6.30	0.00	6.44	7.71	11.95	22.50	198.80
1859	12.70	12.30	22.57	2.41	5.33	1.90	....	....	13.80	8.20	16.20	0.07	198.78
1860	12.90	8.67	5.97	5.90	4.25	0.41	0.87	0.90	4.10	8.59	17.20	....	....
1861	....	15.70	....	....	5.43	....	T.	1.94	1.92	7.90	....	13.80	....
1862	6.58	7.97	20.31	4.10	2.59	3.00	2.35	2.10	8.35	8.40	4.45	6.75	78.95
Means	10.73	11.01	14.60	4.01	5.21	1.97	0.86	1.24	6.92	7.76	12.45	11.36	86.96

FORT DALLES, OREGON.

Year.	Jan.	Feb.	Mar.	Apr.	May.	June.	July.	Aug.	Sept.	Oct.	Nov.	Dec.	Annual.
1850	....	....	....	....	....	....	0.01	0.00	0.00	0.91	1.14	0.19	....
1851	3.81	1.70	1.79	....	....	....	....	....	....	....	....	....	....
1852	....	....	....	....	....	....	....	....	....	0.25	2.75	8.01	....
1853	3.02	1.09	0.27	1.29	0.62	0.90	0.08	0.01	1.41	0.24	4.90	0.95	14.48
1854	2.79	0.73	0.36	1.33	0.00	0.15	0.00	0.18	0.94	1.91	1.41	2.59	12.39
1855	3.63	0.69	1.87	0.17	1.08	0.34	....	0.06	2.69	0.15	1.44	2.84	111.90
1856	....	0.54	0.91	0.79	....	....	....	....	....	....	....	10.79	....
1857	7.08	1.85	2.83	0.00	0.23	1.02	0.58	0.00	2.70	0.25	5.38	7.42	20.34
1858	5.46	8.41	2.81	1.96	1.70	1.93	0.00	0.75	5.16	3.32	6.44	5.93	43.66
1859	5.33	5.90	6.07	....	1.27	0.20	0.06	0.47	5.77	2.14	4.25	3.60	195.96
1860	5.30	2.00	1.33	0.83	1.73	0.34	1.38	0.40	0.35	0.48	3.48	3.47	21.32
1861	3.68	3.28	1.59	1.48	1.34	2.08	0.00	0.14	0.33	0.75	8.97	8.25	28.85
1862	4.47	2.25	3.54	0.20	2.81	1.03	0.22	0.07	0.84	0.43	0.20	0.63	10.70
1863	3.38	2.17	0.62	0.48	0.85	0.71	0.28	0.06	0.30	0.48	0.74	4.11	14.00
1864	5.58	0.72	....	....	0.09	0.36	....	....	0.16	0.27	1.44	2.95	....
1865	....	1.00	1.52	0.06	0.00	0.08	0.55	0.57	0.59	2.06	6.37	2.55	122.18
1866	6.35	2.80	5.56	....	....	....	....	....	....	....	....	....	....
Means	4.52	2.42	2.23	0.74	0.94	0.57	0.34	0.27	1.47	0.97	3.35	4.24	22.00

EAST PORTLAND, OREGON.

Year.	Jan.	Feb.	Mar.	Apr.	May.	June.	July.	Aug.	Sept.	Oct.	Nov.	Dec.	Annual.
1884	*3.70	*4.82	1.18	2.16	0.09	0.12	2.04	0.09	3.06	3.14	4.34	2.37	27.73
1885	3.16	4.06	7.	1.08	1.15	3.11	0.04	0.00	1.13	1.15	4.02	4.13	25.04
1886	5.96	3.00	3.64	3.04	1.08	0.04	0.06	*0.03	0.64	3.12	1.00	11.34	39.87
1887	11.11	9.00	0.34	3.00	1.00	1.06	0.00	0.03	4.08	0.06	4.08	12.30	51.86
Means	5.76	5.40	2.64	2.22	0.83	1.08	0.54	0.02	2.30	1.87	3.36	7.64	33.63

EMPIRE CITY, OREGON.

Year.	Jan.	Feb.	Mar.	Apr.	May.	June.	July.	Aug.	Sept.	Oct.	Nov.	Dec.	Annual.
Means	6.31	7.41	9.11	2.04	1.00	1.28	0.42	0.24	1.24	3.00	4.02	7.25	38.82

NOTE.—The above figures represent averages obtained from five years and ten months record.

EOLA, OREGON.

Year.	Jan.	Feb.	Mar.	Apr.	May.	June.	July.	Aug.	Sept.	Oct.	Nov.	Dec.	Annual.
1870	4.35	6.63	5.77	5.92	1.06	2.26	*0.02	0.08	0.71	0.90	5.06	4.38	36.63
1871	7.12	4.32	7.51	2.24	4.05	0.97	0.33	0.04	1.00	0.66	4.97	7.82	40.91
1872	5.11	13.34	3.87	1.08	1.12	1.18	0.12	0.10	0.79	1.68	3.50	5.97	37.90
1873	6.41	4.45	8.14	3.47	1.30	1.27	0.55	0.03	*1.50	2.27	4.45	*4.50	38.34
1874	8.29	6.35	2.90	3.49	1.29	0.92	*0.18	0.05	1.57	0.30	4.03	3.32	35.80
1875	2.52	0.98	8.40	1.23	2.27	1.40	*0.02	0.38	0.13	6.73	3.38	9.32	42.09
1876	4.14	6.77	5.77	5.37	0.94	1.34	0.09	0.27	1.27	8.01	6.98	0.84	42.37
1877	3.38	5.30	10.66	1.60	0.73	2.41	0.02	0.62	3.62	2.47	13.01	6.21	50.14
1878	6.38	10.22	6.59	1.14	0.87	*0.17	0.55	0.19	3.50	3.93	5.25	2.61	40.77
1879	5.72	10.29	10.96	2.56	5.94	0.47	0.92	1.79	1.54	1.76	4.00	6.03	50.28
1880	7.27	4.29	5.81	2.21	1.06	1.17	0.25	1.30	0.74	1.28	1.81	11.50	37.90
1881	7.79	10.82	3.22	2.59	1.01	1.75	1.27	1.24	1.83	5.92	2.16	3.40	44.17
1882	5.05	9.06	2.72	2.57	1.51	0.91	0.00	0.09	0.82	7.31	3.50	8.76	44.33
1883	7.27	1.81	5.54	5.31	1.62	0.05	0.00	8.00	0.78	3.11	6.23	5.83	36.11
1884	3.46	5.54	2.49	3.09	0.42	1.07	2.20	0.17	0.82	2.80	2.83	6.00	37.44
1885	4.16	7.06	0.55	1.39	3.23	1.40	*0.14	0.06	2.87	1.42	7.36	7.41	36.70
1886	9.48	1.94	3.67	2.74	1.56	0.58	0.24	0.00	1.08	3.12	1.45	6.38	34.92
1887	9.86	4.59	6.41	3.01	3.37	0.89	0.00	0.00	1.87	0.88	3.10	9.29	43.07
Means	5.94	6.24	5.37	2.85	2.00	1.10	0.46	0.37	1.76	3.01	5.05	6.32	40.47

CAMP HARNEY, OREGON.

Year.	Jan.	Feb.	Mar.	Apr.	May.	June.	July.	Aug.	Sept.	Oct.	Nov.	Dec.	Annual.
1867	....	....	....	....	....	....	....	....	....	....	....	3.00	....
1868	1.88	0.27	0.91	0.75	2.01	2.29	0.27	0.00	0.30	0.00	0.64	0.60	9.55
1869	0.97	0.55	1.30	0.86	1.11	0.26	0.31	0.00	0.15	0.00	2.26	0.90	8.47
1870	1.50	0.79	0.59	0.16	*0.70	0.00	0.65	0.00	0.00	0.00	0.09	0.57	4.54
1871	1.97	0.48	2.20	0.06	1.09	0.00	0.04	0.12	0.11	0.03	1.05	2.83	10.58

* Interpolated. ! Incomplete, Schott. T. trace of precipitation.

Statement showing the precipitation in inches and hundredths—Continued.

CAMP HARNEY, OREGON—Continued.

Year.	Jan.	Feb.	Mar.	Apr.	May.	June.	July.	Aug.	Sept.	Oct.	Nov.	Dec.	Annual.
1872	1.89	1.08	0.35	0.10	0.14	0.11	0.00	0.01	0.69	0.83	0.25	0.52	6.31
1873	3.15	1.24	0.39	1.00	0.27	0.58	0.06	0.27	0.34	0.25	1.08	2.41	11.00
1874											2.20	0.34	
1875	1.14	0.45	1.28	0.28	1.15	1.64	0.50	0.02	0.00	1.26	3.00	3.10	13.91
1876	1.81	0.98	1.28	1.11	0.54	0.63	*0.96	0.12	0.07	1.05	0.60	0.48	8.25
1877	1.30	1.35	1.00	0.83	1.76	0.83	0.12	0.54	0.06	0.47	2.78	0.40	13.82
1878	2.00	3.12	1.61	1.73	0.69	0.84	0.30	1.00	0.80	0.76	0.68	0.22	13.81
1879	1.60	1.75	2.04	2.74	1.01	0.80	0.00	*0.03	0.29	0.70	3.34	4.42	18.32
1880	0.56	0.92	0.50	1.70	0.72								
Means	1.51	1.11	1.21	0.98	0.88	0.76	0.35	0.21	0.23	0.49	1.45	1.59	10.87

FORT HOSKINS, OREGON.

Year.	Jan.	Feb.	Mar.	Apr.	May.	June.	July.	Aug.	Sept.	Oct.	Nov.	Dec.	Annual.
1856												18.97	
1857	16.16	10.90	8.63	0.00	1.52	1.80	0.13	0.10	1.65	1.20	7.05	18.72	63.06
1858	7.82	13.29	1.86	2.41	0.92	2.19	0.30	0.21	8.66	8.67	1.50	13.71	67.97
1859	10.70	13.12	15.56	2.41	4.52	0.11	0.06	1.18	7.08	3.48	9.70	4.11	71.04
1860	10.88	4.54	4.05	3.10	3.48	0.06	0.52	0.36	3.70	7.15	10.01	8.83	56.67
1861		8.87	5.33	7.34	3.42	5.00	0.02	0.08	0.55	4.15	18.10	12.00	177.30
1862	8.97	4.23	13.77	3.10	1.08	2.80	0.84	0.96	1.67	1.74	0.94	7.00	45.70
1863	10.85	10.40	7.23	0.27	0.83	0.25	0.75	0.30	2.85	2.96	6.73	13.50	74.64
1864	13.48	2.60	11.08	4.00	1.25	1.35	0.50	0.65	2.50				163.81
Means	12.47	9.34	8.44	2.80	2.85	1.80	0.30	0.36	3.24	3.90	8.58	11.37	85.32

FORT KLAMATH, OREGON.

Year.	Jan.	Feb.	Mar.	Apr.	May.	June.	July.	Aug.	Sept.	Oct.	Nov.	Dec.	Annual.
1864	2.16	4.50	4.00	6.20	1.50	0.00	*0.30	1.40			1.61	2.51	
1865	7.36	2.45	5.94							1.40	7.39	5.00	136.96
1866										0.90	2.20		
1872								0.00	2.30	0.02	1.20	2.89	
1873	2.96	1.88	2.37	0.96	0.51	0.87	0.60	0.54	1.39	5.47	0.71	118.05	
1874		0.28	2.50	0.98	1.88	0.86	0.30	0.42	0.00	4.61	8.57	7.13	
1875	2.46	2.78	3.21	2.16	0.74	1.02	0.42	0.16	1.05	4.06	1.78	0.12	18.90
1876	1.74	3.18	5.78	0.46	1.72	1.28	0.30	0.06	0.14	1.28	5.10	1.06	22.72
1877	8.86	3.04	5.16	0.50	0.50	*0.84	0.28	0.80	0.86	1.20	1.24	0.82	20.02
1878	2.34	2.00	4.15	1.42	2.45	0.26	0.29	0.47	0.30	0.90	5.78	6.14	26.40
1879	2.34	0.92	1.50	2.77	1.24	0.38	0.20	0.08	0.00	0.00		1.92	
1880	8.42	4.14	*1.30	1.10	0.10	*1.14	1.34	0.30	0.68	3.04	2.78	3.00	27.24
1881	2.40	4.38	1.48	2.72	1.38	*0.42	0.88	0.00	0.80	2.10	1.68	3.90	23.15
1882	2.31	0.33	0.25	0.95	1.49	0.80	T.	0.10	0.18	0.67	0.63	5.43	11.04
1883	2.71	4.64	3.02	1.76	0.72	3.23	0.11	0.00	0.83	1.15	a6.77	4.98	
1884	2.31	3.14	0.47	1.06	1.58	1.38	0.00	*0.00	0.86	0.43	7.29	4.99	22.81
1885	7.30	1.17	3.69	2.77	1.12	b0.83	1.38	0.02	0.00	1.54	0.70	0.55	27.08
1887	5.64	5.98	0.86	1.80	0.85	0.40	0.70	0.57	0.34	0.32	1.66	4.33	23.45
Means	3.72	2.85	2.84	1.42	1.19	0.77	0.46	6.31	0.55	1.57	3.25	3.66	22.50

LA GRANDE, OREGON.

Year.	Jan.	Feb.	Mar.	Apr.	May.	June.	July.	Aug.	Sept.	Oct.	Nov.	Dec.	Annual.
1886						0.62	0.18	0.10	0.40	1.50	1.77	4.64	
1887	5.18	0.70	2.25	1.39	0.66	2.90	0.33	0.49	0.55	0.51	1.22	3.73	19.81
Means	5.18	0.70	2.95	1.39	0.66	1.71	0.26	0.30	0.48	1.00	1.24	4.19	10.16

LAKEVIEW, OREGON.

Year.	Jan.	Feb.	Mar.	Apr.	May.	June.	July.	Aug.	Sept.	Oct.	Nov.	Dec.	Annual.
1882											0.34	2.67	
1884	2.70	2.49	4.12	2.35	*1.56	6.58	0.00	1.18	1.82	1.63	0.02	1.29	26.34
1885	2.36	*2.00	0.20	0.62	1.47	*1.40	0.25	0.43	0.92	0.32	5.57	2.15	18.09
1886	2.15	1.26	0.95	1.22	0.97	1.02	0.11	0.00	0.01	1.51	0.65	3.13	14.07
1887	2.15	2.28	1.06	1.80	1.06	1.38	e0.30	0.54	0.09	c0.01	d0.32	1.51	13.44
Means	2.50	2.00	1.58	1.60	1.25	3.58	0.32	0.54	0.51	0.87	1.58	2.15	17.57

LINKVILLE, OREGON.

Year.	Jan.	Feb.	Mar.	Apr.	May.	June.	July.	Aug.	Sept.	Oct.	Nov.	Dec.	Annual.
1884	0.50	2.13	3.13	2.44	#1.72	2.27	0.38	0.00	0.58	1.77	0.15	2.07	17.04
1885	2.23	2.33	0.61	3.85	1.68	*1.39	T.	0.00	*0.96	0.75	3.75	2.35	18.71
1886	5.31	1.21	1.53	1.50	1.37	1.18	1.51	0.00	0.00	1.53	0.65	2.27	18.06
1887	2.16	1.47	0.40	1.50	0.54	0.04	0.51	0.42	0.05	T.	0.72	1.86	10.77
Means	2.56	1.78	1.44	2.10	1.32	1.42	0.58	0.10	0.37	1.02	1.32	2.34	10.27

* Interpolated.   † Incomplete, Schott.   T. trace of precipitation.   a 17 days.   b 25 days.   c 20 days.   d 26 days.   e 23 days.

*Statement showing the precipitation in inches and hundredths—*Continued.

MOUNT ANGEL, OREGON.

Year.	Jan.	Feb.	Mar.	Apr.	May.	June.	July.	Aug.	Sept.	Oct.	Nov.	Dec.	Annual.
1896						4.36	4.68	0.00	1.92	4.39	2.84	12.45	
1897	15.36	3.72	10.30	6.93	4.42	2.29	0.00	0.33	2.35	2.00	*4.00	*14.21	66.91
Means	15.36	3.72	10.30	6.93	4.42	3.32	2.34	0.16	2.14	3.20	3.42	13.33	66.64

OREGON CITY, OREGON.

1851	13.83	3.43	5.96	3.13	4.58	0.40	0.00	1.90	1.96	4.58	4.09	7.70	51.26
1857				0.79	2.54	1.80	0.35	0.48	0.72	1.38	6.68	8.63	†43.05
1858	4.05	3.81	4.87	1.63	2.09	2.04	0.10	0.44	4.04	4.55	4.44	9.93	43.09
1850	8.19	8.29	10.72										
Means	7.93	5.17	7.15	1.92	3.37	1.41	0.15	0.94	2.24	3.46	5.12	8.75	47.81

PORT ORFORD, OREGON.

1852						0.33	0.81	1.00			12.03	16.01	
1853	11.81	6.65	6.45	6.11	1.67		0.00		2.56	0.19	11.10	4.50	6.37
1854								0.10	4.49	2.52	14.18	20.00	†62.75
1855	7.81	6.04	9.81	5.17	8.80	1.90	1.35						
1856	7.62	4.07	2.31	11.30	3.20	1.85	1.38						
Means	9.08	5.79	6.17	7.53	4.56	1.38	0.56	1.22	2.34	7.81	10.27	14.48	70.50

PORTLAND, OREGON.

1858				1.35	1.51	0.13							
1859		8.05	7.85	1.44	1.51	0.13	0.22	0.97					
1870	4.85	4.30	4.30	6.30	1.95	1.85	0.20	0.29	0.45	0.58	6.05	4.40	32.56
1871	7.80	5.06	9.81	3.64	5.18	0.50	0.55	0.45	1.15	1.19	2.77	7.62	45.35
1872	8.56	12.13	5.28	2.96	0.92	1.52	0.20	0.13	1.26	1.80	4.67	9.47	46.98
1873	8.49	8.56	12.76	2.35	2.16	0.96	1.02	0.84	0.00	3.96	4.38	5.15	50.52
1874	9.48	4.28	5.15	3.68	2.36	2.68	0.19	0.68	1.70	0.36	10.22	5.24	46.17
1875	4.49	1.98	9.41	2.10	2.87	2.05	0.02	0.53	0.71	6.73	15.77	13.41	60.06
1876	4.80	7.50	9.12	5.34	1.88	2.35	0.96	0.56	1.09	10.53	10.08	6.68	55.04
1877	2.76	7.56	11.31	3.44	2.24	2.05	0.54	1.70	3.96	5.03	12.45	6.67	56.30
1878	6.87	12.16	6.23	1.85	2.17	0.13	1.10	0.50	3.54	3.22	5.61	4.82	47.70
1879	5.28	13.22	11.70	2.19	0.60	2.16	1.75	0.07	2.18	4.23	4.58	7.38	62.22
1880	12.27	8.67	4.46	2.92	3.13	1.80	0.99	1.31	1.34	1.47	3.17	13.93	51.67
1881	9.57	13.36	2.89	3.51	1.38	2.34	1.19	2.11	2.64	4.90	6.91	8.64	58.05
1882	5.06	10.48	2.53	4.80	1.81	1.01	0.95	0.07	0.01	11.03	7.11	20.14	87.24
1883	13.71	2.34	8.40	7.88	1.67	0.08	8.00	0.18	0.67	3.91	8.26	8.34	51.45
1884	3.70	4.86	2.25	3.57	1.34	1.42	1.80	0.33	4.25	4.01	3.24	7.62	38.31
1885	4.67	6.72	0.93	1.12	4.89	1.77	0.24	0.00	2.48	1.88	8.52	7.17	39.50
1886	9.23	1.96	6.20	3.16	1.10	0.67	0.32	0.08	1.19	2.87	1.00	11.82	38.76
1887	12.31	2.81	4.00	5.06	4.77	1.44	0.03	0.88	8.08	1.34	8.43	11.34	54.17
Means	7.25	6.95	6.60	3.27	2.58	1.49	0.82	0.64	1.78	3.94	6.56	8.31	49.90

ROSEBURGH, OREGON.

1877	8.70	7.30	6.36	0.79	1.02	0.39	0.75	0.25	1.40	2.76	8.76	4.96	
1878	4.74	4.21	6.80	3.97	4.63	0.58	1.18	0.46	1.29	2.55	3.55	2.73	36.02
1879	6.37	2.49	2.81	3.98	1.30	0.68	0.15	1.47	1.15	3.20	5.79	7.98	45.03
1880	11.88	8.19	1.95	1.07	0.73	2.92	0.41	0.46	0.47	6.77	0.77	6.30	31.44
1881	4.21	8.21	2.83	5.14	0.85	0.61	0.79	0.00	0.73	3.96	1.15	5.14	48.66
1882	2.98	1.17	1.79	3.87	2.29	0.01	0.85	0.00	1.86	3.92	1.15	9.84	34.77
1883	3.06	3.71	3.27	3.48	0.85	1.00	0.01	0.01	0.62	2.84	3.20	5.73	22.48
1884	2.99	3.29	0.28	1.21	2.91	1.59	0.03	a 0.03	*1.38	1.15	0.78	9.30	32.58
1885	7.50	2.44	3.03	4.98	1.11	0.13	0.07	T.	0.30	1.66	8.10	8.52	30.91
1886	8.64	6.24	2.98	2.79	1.43	0.80	3.20	T.	0.83	8.43	2.83	7.30	36.17
1887							0.07	0.09	0.51	1.13	3.10	8.89	37.84
Means	6.45	4.72	3.33	3.10	1.79	0.96	0.86	0.29	0.87	2.66	3.73	6.95	35.13

FORT STEVENS, OREGON.

1865											16.53	16.70	
1866	12.00	7.20	10.75	5.80	4.85				0.95	7.98	11.35	16.90	†87.29
1867	15.50	13.77	3.86	5.70	0.58	1.67	4.84	0.20	3.54	8.28	7.30	21.90	85.82
1868	1.30	4.75	0.24	6.95	3.83	2.72	0.31	0.00	0.31				†52.33
1869				5.27	0.85	0.36							

*Interpolated. |Incomplete, Schott.   a 16 days.   T. trace of precipitation.

Statement showing the precipitation in inches and hundredths—Continued.

FORT STEVENS, OREGON—Continued.

Year.	Jan.	Feb.	Mar.	Apr.	May.	June.	July.	Aug.	Sept.	Oct.	Nov.	Dec.	Annual.
1871	*20.00	*10.60	*17.06	*4.00	*3.00	*1.00	0.81	0.16	1.82	1.78	12.09	13.90	85.48
1872	6.50	15.28	8.57	5.00	4.60	6.90	3.90	0.26	5.36	3.27	9.78	10.90	81.00
1873	14.75	10.28	20.76	3.40	1.87	5.52	1.55	2.75	0.95	3.91	6.96	6.35	78.03
1874	16.96	12.06	6.05	5.66	4.04	5.90	1.40	2.65	4.78	1.89	13.72	8.55	85.40
1875	7.45	3.46	15.06	3.31	7.44	1.96	0.77	1.02	2.68	14.13	17.56	13.62	87.61
1876	11.57	11.12	12.38	7.25	5.16	2.45	2.37	1.96	2.09	11.66	17.15	2.83	87.96
1877	3.77	6.94	16.11	2.38	4.02	2.99	2.06	3.69	5.61	8.51	22.71	6.42	83.61
1878	6.73	12.34	3.02	2.37	2.90	0.99	2.00	6.64	6.42	6.30	11.77	4.53	56.86
1879	7.34	19.19	22.60	3.95	5.20	3.30	5.95	1.95	4.40	7.01	6.66	17.73	107.50
1880	28.06	7.38	8.53	4.83	4.91	3.15	2.07	6.80	2.04	4.62	4.54	21.27	97.88
1881	14.69	15.00	6.18	4.67	4.11	6.14	1.20	2.89	1.71	11.39	7.68	13.47	91.47
1882	6.96	13.27	5.00	5.08	1.09	1.87	1.15	1.82	*1.80	10.98	8.42	9.28	66.14
1883	5.41	8.26	......	......	......	......	......	......	......	......	......	......	......
Means	11.85	10.67	10.82	4.72	8.58	3.09	2.08	1.88	2.90	7.23	11 75	11.85	81.96

THE DALLES, OREGON.

1875	4.17	0.31	2.13	0.50	0.81	1.63	0.14	0.12	0.72	4.80	6.16	4.60	26.40
1876	2.78	1.39	2.26	1.09	0.20	0.34	0.97	0.02	0.13	2.37	4.31	0.46	15.34
1877	0.78	1.60	3.60	1.21	1.09	0.15	6.28	0.10	1.24	1.90	4.18	1.56	17.89
1878	2.96	2.32	1.99	0.20	0.26	0.02	0.06	0.13	1.01	1.59	1.42	1.61	13.53
1879	1.42	5.32	3.15	1.34	2.94	0.11	0.31	0.48	0.76	0.68	1.34	2.57	21.55
1880	2.04	1.33	0.16	1.98	0.94	0.03	0.02	0.43	0.06	0.12	0.69	2.75	13.61
1881	6.37	6.23	0.38	1.29	0.14	1.82	0.11	0.28	0.36	2.67	0.75	1.67	21.92
1882	1.48	2.06	0.23	0.53	0.27	0.60	0.13	0.72	0.43	2.30	0.15	5.14	15.53
1883	4.83	0.61	2.32	1.22	0.54	0.01	0.00	0.20	0.01	0.46	2.19	1.77	14.15
1884	1.33	3.10	0.74	1.33	0.04	0.96	0.44	0.12	0.65	1.27	0.82	7.04	17.81
1885	1.10	2.88	0.14	0.31	0.81	1.01	0.10	0.03	0.87	0.28	1.78	2.64	11.95
1886	5.45	0.53	0.03	0.30	0.11	0.07	0.19	0.02	0.14	0.61	0.21	5.01	13.80
1887	6.01	1.13	0.73	0.40	0.32	0.67	0.07	0.18	0.36	0.15	1.06	0.61	12.21
Means	2.86	2.27	1.43	0.84	0.65	0.57	0.15	0.21	0.62	1.48	1.96	3.39	10.55

UMATILLA, OREGON.

1877								0.02	0.50	0.68	1.92	0.64	......
1878	1.14	1.26	1.72	0.01	0.36	0.02	0.32	0.15	1.14	0.56	0.73	0.38	7.76
1879	0.95	1.81	1.30	1.49	1.96	0.26	0.21	0.23	0.83	0.33	0.61	0.78	10.58
1880	0.54	0.54	0.36	0.97	0.57	0.38	0.48	1.14	0.18	0.35	0.54	5.55	9.71
1881	2.45	1.92	0.44	0.89	0.06	0.96	0.53	0.73	0.74	1.54	0.96	0.45	11.06
1882	0.71	0.73	0.32	0.76	0.26	0.17	0.04	0.00	1.70	1.79	0.61	1.06	8.75
1883	2.50	0.57	1.26	......	......	......	......	......	......	......	......	......	......
Means	1.40	1.14	0.96	0.82	0.64	0.36	0.32	0.34	0.78	0.88	0.90	1.31	9.61

FORT UMPQUA, OREGON.

1856								0.00	0.00	0.00	4.91	11.48	......
1857	13.53	11.44	6.41	0.67	3.07	2.98	0.00	0.10	1.50	2.16	4.46	12.80	62.95
1858	11.70	10.40	7.80	4.62	3.75	0.85	0.20	0.80	2.24	7.05	9.17	14.69	72.17
1859	9.06	15.35	14.45	2.22	3.19	0.85	0.40	1.13	5.30	2.00	8.56	4.73	66.16
1860	7.66	6.77	4.20	5.72	2.92	0.30	0.80	0.18	2.23	5.95	11.09	6.73	55.53
1861	11.50	16.49	7.40	7.47	4.30	6.02	0.00	5.25	1.15	3.88	18.05	18.95	90.46
1862	8.21	6.62	16.09	3.33	1.46	......	......	......	......	......	......	......	......
Means	10.28	9.61	9.72	4.00	3.09	2.18	0.30	0.38	2.27	3.66	9.79	11.66	67.35

CAMP WARNER, OREGON.

1868								0.00					
1869						0.78	0.86	0.00	0.58	0.90	2.66	1.57	......
1870	1.50	1.39	0.88	1.30	1.78	0.81	0.05	0.09	0.00	0.60	1.40	2.39	11.79
1871	1.40	3.44	0.76	0.95	1.92	0.14	0.11	0.07	0.90	0.35	0.83	5.63	13.34
1872	1.49	1.61	0.70	0.96	3.23	0.36	0.60	0.90	1.76	0.35	1.75	2.78	17.67
1873	1.57	2.16	0.65	1.96	1.49	0.37	0.85	0.19	0.30	0.77	1.88	2.06	14.26
1874	2.52	1.66	2.28	1.22	1.00	1.35	0.00	......	......	......	......	......	......
Means	1.81	1.96	1.21	1.21	1.88	0.64	0.28	0.19	0.60	0.23	1.70	2.80	14.43

* Interpolated.

Statement showing the precipitation in inches and hundredths—Continued.

CAMP WATSON, OREGON.

Year.	Jan.	Feb.	Mar.	Apr.	May.	June.	July.	Aug.	Sept.	Oct.	Nov.	Dec.	Annual.
1867						0.10	0.22			0.94	0.35	0.02	3.69	
1868	10.14	1.19	0.02	1.39	1.21	3.70	0.06	0.60	0.30	0.21	0.64	2.54	†14.36
1869	1.72	0.52	1.78										
Means	0.93	0.86	1.35	1.36	1.21	1.94	0.11	0.00	0.62	0.28	0.76	3.12	13.12

FORT YAMHILL, OREGON.

Year.	Jan.	Feb.	Mar.	Apr.	May.	June.	July.	Aug.	Sept.	Oct.	Nov.	Dec.	Annual.
1856										6.43	14.90		
1857	11.86	0.03	8.52	8.10	1.76	1.28	0.06	0.10	1.68	1.86	7.58	14.26	57.78
1858	8.18	9.37	7.51	2.06	3.37	2.54	0.90	0.16	4.62	4.47	6.85	11.37	62.00
1859	9.35	10.57	11.67	1.50	2.60	0.09	0.94	1.68	5.75	3.10	8.02	1.86	55.63
1860	8.63	4.62	4.53	4.06	3.74	0.46	0.40	0.42	3.16	5.75	8.01	7.13	56.91
1861	10.09	7.68	4.01	8.06	3.70	5.92	8.00	0.28	6.55	4.29	*7.55	13.17	63.79
1862	12.56	8.65	14.19	4.37	1.78	1.51	0.55	0.20	1.25	2.45	0.90	7.41	58.76
1863	11.02	10.92	3.79	3.51	2.65	0.43	1.92	0.25	2.28	2.37	5.58	10.01	53.78
1864	7.61	1.72	6.55	2.03	0.80	1.54	0.31	0.50	1.85	1.30	8.19	9.95	42.95
1865	5.93	4.74	8.00	1.60	1.06	0.75	0.90	0.78	3.66	1.35	16.27	10.80	54.70
1866	8.91	4.75	8.69	3.50									
Means	9.51	7.30	7.66	2.99	2.44	1.01	0.36	0.42	2.69	2.96	7.55	10.08	56.27

BOISÉ CITY, IDAHO.

Year.	Jan.	Feb.	Mar.	Apr.	May.	June.	July.	Aug.	Sept.	Oct.	Nov.	Dec.	Annual.
1877						0.35	0.09	0.27	0.85	2.05	0.01		
1878	3.73	2.18	1.63	0.37	1.18	0.86	0.31	0.50	0.27	0.30	0.53	0.35	10.21
1879	3.82	1.42	3.04	1.42	0.92	1.43	T.	0.03	0.14	0.76	1.20	1.65	17.63
1880	0.90	0.94	0.50	1.50	1.57	0.11	0.02	0.42	0.11	0.50	0.48	4.01	10.06
1881	3.62	3.51	6.64	1.34	0.07	0.29	0.13	0.00	0.26	2.12	0.94	0.45	13.56
1882	1.62	1.73	1.54	2.33	0.34	0.29		0.00	1.36	2.94	0.08	2.20	14.43
1883	2.77	1.20	0.28	0.61	2.12	0.20	T.	T.	0.20	4.06	0.46	2.27	
1884	1.75	1.32	2.78	0.78	4.62	3.41	0.60	0.07	2.11	1.52	0.13	5.67	21.95
1885	1.50	2.29	0.03	0.09	3.14	1.08	0.23	0.09	0.39	0.58	2.07	1.07	12.56
1886	2.90	0.94	0.82	2.43	0.61	0.44	0.24	T.	T.	0.72	0.43	2.64	12.23
1887	2.89	1.13	1.33	1.54	8.51	1.58	0.12	0.20	0.14	0.03	0.04	1.74	11.34
1888	1.64	0.60	0.51	0.12	0.94								
Means	2.35	1.56	1.19	2.05	1.12	0.97	0.20	8.10	0.48	1.31	0.76	2.21	14.30

* Interpolated.   † Incomplete, Schott.   T. trace of precipitation.

APPENDIX No. 2.

Precipitation data for Washington Territory.

Name of station	County	Latitude	Longitude	Elevation	Record Length	Record From	Record To (inclusive)	Remarks as to observers and character of records
		° ′	° ′	Feet.	Yrs. Mos.			
Almota	Whitman	46 44	117 00		3 0	Jan., 1881	Dec., 1888	Signal Service.
Bellingham, Fort	Whatcom	48 45	122 30	68	2 2	June, 1857	July, 1859	United States post hospital.
Cape Disappointment (Fort Canby).	Pacific	46 17	124 03	20	21 3	July, 1864	May, 1888	July, 1861, to Aug., 1883, United States post hospital. Sept., 1883, to May, 1888, Signal Service.
Cascades, Fort	Skamania	45 39	121 50		3 1	May, 1858	May, 1861	United States post hospital.
Cathlamet	Wahkiakum	46 15	123 32	40	4 3	Dec., 1871	Aug., 1876	Charles McCall.
Colfax	Whitman	46 54	117 9		2 5	Jan., 1881	May, 1883	Signal Service.
Colville, Fort	Stevens	48 42	118 02	1,963	18 1	Dec., 1859	Feb., 1880	United States post hospital.
Dayton	Columbia	46 19	117 56	1,683	6 0	Dec., 1879	Nov., 1885	Signal Service.
Ediz Hook Light Station (Port Angeles).	Clallam	48 8	123 24	12	7 4	Jan., 1881	May, 1888	Jan., 1881, to Nov., 1883, Thomas Stratton. Dec., 1883, to May, 1888, Signal Service.
Kennewick	Yakima	46 15	119 15	350	3 1	Nov., 1884	Nov., 1887	A. W. Gray.
Neah Bay	Clallam	48 22	124 37	40	11 9	May, 1863	Dec., 1887	May, 1863, to Dec., 1881, J. G. Swan. Dec., 1883, to Dec., 1887, Signal Service.
New Tacoma	Pierce	47 16	122 26	296	4 0	Jan., 1884	Dec., 1887	E. N. Fuller.
Olympia	Thurston	47 3	122 53	36	10 11	July, 1877	May, 1888	Signal Service.
Pleasant Grove	Kittitass	47 9	120 30	1,500	2 4	Jan., 1884	Apr., 1886	George W. Parrish.
Pomeroy	Garfield	46 30	117 0		2 1	June, 1881	June, 1883	Signal Service.
Makely, Port	Kitsap	47 32	122 40	30	10 0	Jan., 1878	Dec., 1887	R. M. Hoskinson.
Port Townsend	Jefferson	48 07	122 45	8	4 11	Nov., 1867	Mar., 1877	United States post hospital.
Pyalt	Clallam	48 10	124 0	7	4 1	Dec., 1883	Dec., 1887	Signal Service.
San Juan Island	San Juan	48 29	123 07	150	14 0	Feb., 1860	Dec., 1874	United States post hospital.
Seattle	King	47 32	122 32	20	1 1	June, 1877	June, 1878	R. M. Hoskinson.
Semiahmoo, Camp	Whatcom	49 01	122 47	11	1 4	Mar., 1859	June, 1860	United States post hospital.
Simcoe, Fort	Yakima	46 30	120 49		2 1	Apr., 1857	Apr., 1859	Do.
Spokane, Fort	Spokane	47 30	118 30	1,600	4 10	Mar., 1883	Dec., 1887	Mar. to Sept., 1883, United States post hospital. Oct., 1883, to Aug., 1887, signal Service. Sept. to Dec., 1887, United States post hospital.
Spokane, Falls	do	49 4	117 25	1,999	7 0	Jan., 1881	Dec., 1887	Signal Service.
Steilacoom, Fort	Pierce	47 11	122 34	300	13 9	Nov., 1849	Mar., 1863	United States post hospital.
Tatoosh Island Light House.	Clallam	48 23	124 44	90	6 11	Apr., 1869	Dec., 1887	Apr., 1869, to Jan., 1872, A. Sampson. Oct., 1883, to Dec., 1887, Signal Service.
Townsend, Fort	Jefferson	48 05	122 46	135	14 0	Jan., 1860	Dec., 1887	United States post hospital.
Vancouver, Fort	Clarke	45 40	122 36	50	17 1	Dec., 1849	July, 1868	Do.
Walla Walla	Walla Walla	46 05	118 54	900	4 1	Dec., 1850	Dec., 1887	Dec., 1869, to Jan., 1870, A. H. Simmons. Feb., 1877, to Nov., 1879, J. Straight. Dec., 1885, to Dec., 1887, Signal Service.
Walla Walla, Fort	do	46 03	118 20		15 4	Jan., 1857	Dec., 1887	United States post hospital.
Melosa, Mont	Lewis and Clarke	46 34	112 4	4,000	7 11	Apr., 1880	May, 1-88	Signal Service.

Statement showing the precipitation in inches and hundredths—Continued.

ALMOTA, WASH.

Year.	Jan.	Feb.	Mar.	Apr.	May	June.	July.	Aug.	Sept.	Oct.	Nov.	Dec.	Annual.
1881	*4.80	*4.06	1.20	1.66	0.60	6.70	0.79	0.14	2.17	1.95	1.20	1.40	20.70
1882	0.45	2.88	0.97	2.71	0.94	6.01	0.60	0.06	0.05	3.37	1.44	2.51	15.96
1883	1.15	0.28	1.74	0.05	1.57	6.05	*0.00	*0.30	*0.10	*1.64	*2.00	*2.00	11.78
Means	2.13	2.39	1.29	1.77	1.04	6.25	0.46	0.15	0.77	2.32	1.55	2.00	16.12

FORT BELLINGHAM, WASH.

	Jan.	Feb.	Mar.	Apr.	May	June.	July.	Aug.	Sept.	Oct.	Nov.	Dec.	Annual.
1857						0.75	0.33	0.24	2.61	2.02	2.70	6.92	
1858	3.72	8.43	2.74	2.09	1.21	1.35	0.42	2.10	1.06	2.39	4.03	5.49	31.29
1859	2.36	1.78	4.29	1.92	1.94	1.48	0.54						
Means	3.04	2.00	3.52	2.10	1.58	1.19	0.43	1.20	2.24	2.20	3.36	6.20	29.66

PORT BLAKELY (BAINBRIDGE ISLAND), WASH.

	Jan.	Feb.	Mar.	Apr.	May	June.	July.	Aug.	Sept.	Oct.	Nov.	Dec.	Annual.
1878	*5.68	10.22	5.47	2.15	3.25	0.36	0.78	0.20	3.55	2.61	9.27	5.27	49.09
1879	5.85	9.70	13.70	4.44	5.00	3.35	2.55	1.82	2.45	5.11	4.40	6.55	64.87
1880	11.05	4.06	4.15	2.15	3.70	2.21	0.48	1.30	0.85	1.90	0.85	17.25	49.95
1881	6.55	10.30	7.05	3.19	1.62	1.20	1.47	2.45	0.75	5.00	5.07	8.00	53.82
1882	4.31	6.96	3.42	4.24	1.92	1.52	2.00	0.31	0.95	4.06	5.35	7.35	42.19
1883	5.45	2.45	2.80	5.96	1.90	0.12	0.28	0.06	1.80	3.30	3.71	5.05	34.85
1884	4.60	5.53	0.97	2.50	0.58	2.70	0.19	1.35	2.48	0.20	2.55	5.55	34.88
1885	10.10	5.40	0.77	0.25	3.35	0.25	0.82	0.01	4.27	4.46	8.04	6.22	43.08
1886	6.95	1.96	2.78	2.37	1.76	0.41	1.22	0.35	1.21	3.00	1.80	11.15	34.97
1887	3.51	3.35	8.80	3.06	3.42	1.15	0.16	0.02	2.81	1.45	5.01	7.93	40.97
Means	6.42	5.98	5.08	3.08	2.59	1.34	0.99	0.79	2.11	3.76	4.78	8.03	44.00

CAPE DISAPPOINTMENT, OR FORT CANBY, WASH.

	Jan.	Feb.	Mar.	Apr.	May	June.	July.	Aug.	Sept.	Oct.	Nov.	Dec.	Annual.
1864	10.26	4.37	13.25	3.80	3.40	1.60	0.52	0.37	4.98	1.72		10.00	
1865						1.20				3.70	13.90		170.74
1866										1.62	7.12	10.12	
1867	12.14	12.19	1.06	5.32	6.93	2.40	7.90	0.50	3.90	14.80	11.50	18.20	81.74
1868	4.50	4.50	13.50	8.20	4.20	4.60		0.00	0.40	6.10	10.40	14.60	174.60
1869	15.60	4.80	6.20	6.15									
1871	*20.00	*10.90	*15.00	*3.00	0.76	10.50	0.50	0.10	2.50	2.10	5.02	11.11	72.50
1872	7.54	12.75	8.20	5.84	1.46	1.17	0.98	*0.80	*1.00	*1.50	*2.80	*10.06	54.04
1873	5.61	6.81	9.37	1.07	0.70	1.60	*1.00	*1.50	*0.80	*1.00	*2.20	7.10	38.05
1874	14.54	10.82	4.12	3.55	3.90	0.25	2.90	2.50	2.75	1.00	11.29	6.68	86.50
1875	4.19	4.85	15.68	3.67	9.02	0.73	0.05	1.34	1.12	7.81	14.92	10.18	73.36
1876	8.94	8.90	8.28	7.02	8.96	2.15	1.72	1.96	1.32	8.50	13.32	2.80	87.43
1877	4.48	8.06	12.96	2.96	2.42	2.72	1.72	2.64	8.42	6.00	17.60	7.58	77.06
1878	10.80	13.94	8.98	2.16	2.64	0.58	1.94	1.14	5.56	4.50	8.36	5.38	61.08
1879	*8.24	15.08	10.92	2.74	3.76	1.75	5.06	1.98	2.98	7.47	5.60	10.82	70.41
1880	23.28	7.96	6.66	4.09	5.22	2.58	2.56	0.78	1.80	3.96	3.58	13.54	74.61
1881	9.64	13.34	7.58	5.51	3.22	3.15	2.46	0.90	2.50	9.34	7.20	11.55	76.69
1882	7.19	10.48	8.40	6.80	2.18	1.84	0.98	0.93	2.68	10.98	8.42	12.46	80.88
1883	0.38	8.60	2.44	6.52	8.14	T.	T.	T.	3.15	5.65	8.34	8.87	
1884	6.45	5.20	2.18	2.96	1.30	2.16	1.73	1.25	6.26	8.24	4.05	5.91	48.71
1885	6.68	11.20	1.15	7.12	3.45	3.33	0.22	0.12	3.43	3.48	13.72	10.56	58.40
1886	6.33	4.77	8.26	5.44	3.43	2.67	3.33	1.07	3.14	5.24	4.47	17.88	85.60
1887	11.91	8.29	14.13	6.38	4.89	0.95	0.33	0.16	3.62	2.73	7.25	15.18	72.81
1888	11.89	3.00	6.58	3.53	0.40								
Means	9.83	8.54	8.06	4.56	3.02	2.17	1.84	0.90	3.02	5.40	9.16	10.60	67.50

FORT CASCADES, WASH.

	Jan.	Feb.	Mar.	Apr.	May	June.	July.	Aug.	Sept.	Oct.	Nov.	Dec.	Annual.
1858					4.05	3.49	0.60	1.00	7.35	5.78	8.36	8.18	
1859	7.72	8.54	13.83	8.14	2.43	0.63	0.16	1.06	2.75	4.38	7.20	4.13	50.97
1860	7.96	6.61	2.90	3.48	6.52	1.34	1.24	0.76	1.86	6.30	12.95	5.80	55.77
1861	10.50	11.06	5.66	8.87	5.44								
Means	8.56	8.74	7.47	5.16	4.51	1.70	0.47	0.97	5.65	5.15	9.48	6.65	54.00

* Interpolated.   ‡ Incomplete, Schott.   T. trace of precipitation.

Statement showing the precipitation in inches and hundredths,—Continued.

CATHLAMET, WASH.

Year.	Jan.	Feb.	Mar.	Apr.	May.	June.	July.	Aug.	Sept.	Oct.	Nov.	Dec.	Annual.
1871						1.80	0.50	0.50	1.40	2.18	8.30	13.80	
1872												7.70	
1873	15.80	8.50	18.00	4.80	1.00	2.10	1.30	1.40	0.50	3.88	*4.50	*5.50	85.30
1874	14.30	7.60	8.20	3.00	3.60	4.50	8.30	2.90	2.40		13.20	6.20	169.19
1875	8.30	4.50	18.50	5.70	5.80	2.40	0.80	1.70	1.80	8.50	13.00	20.01	00.61
1876	9.50	0.90	13.20	6.50	4.20	4.00	1.00	1.80					
Means	11.98	7.09	13.98	4.95	3.68	2.92	0.84	1.66	1.52	4.73	9.25	10.48	72.99

COLFAX, WASH.

Year.	Jan.	Feb.	Mar.	Apr.	May.	June.	July.	Aug.	Sept.	Oct.	Nov.	Dec.	Annual.
1881	*5.00	*4.00	*1.00	1.07	0.77	1.08	1.20	0.02	1.86	2.75	2.50	2.79	25.13
1882	2.84	3.49	1.70	3.02	1.20	0.12	0.30	0.03	0.02	6.81	1.60	6.42	28.15
1883	4.32	1.16	1.73	2.32	1.20								
Means	4.05	2.88	1.48	2.34	1.06	0.60	0.75	0.32	1.14	4.78	2.10	4.60	20.10

FORT COLVILLE, WASH.

Year.	Jan.	Feb.	Mar.	Apr.	May.	June.	July.	Aug.	Sept.	Oct.	Nov.	Dec.	Annual.
1859											1.47	2.38	
1860	2.20	2.23	0.80	a 0.26	a 2.37	a 2.05	a 0.07	0.85	1.57	2.09	1.70		
1861	2.02	1.80	1.63	0.13	2.83	2.46	0.06	0.14	0.64	0.93	1.40		15.50
1862	1.07	0.90	blk.	0.13	2.08	1.73	2.89	0.10	0.38	0.84	3.00	1.21	14.05
1863	0.14	2.00	T	blk.	0.19	0.64	0.08	0.07	0.18	0.14	0.03	0.10	13.96
1864	0.08	0.08	0.06	0.05	0.05	0.38	0.05						
1866										1.29	2.55	2.97	
1867	2.46	1.42	0.05	0.23	1.17	1.06	4.70	0.10	0.45	1.04	1.53	14.30	†14.65
1868	0.54	10.02	10.02	10.13	1.10	2.18	0.07	0.20	0.80	0.85	1.08	1.80	
1869	0.48	10.02	1.48	1.50	(!)1.00	0.49	1.20	1.91		0.00	8.94	3.07	118.15
1870	3.80	1.74	1.23	2.84	2.08	1.11	1.80	0.54	0.24	0.78	1.90	2.46	20.27
1871	2.48	2.08	2.40	1.52	2.54	1.86	1.06	1.16	0.86	0.36	4.24	4.00	24.43
1872	5.33	2.67	1.55	0.24	0.86	0.28	0.50	0.92	0.85	0.33	0.41	1.16	117.45
1873	0.97	1.35	1.47	1.24	1.08	0.82	0.40	8.86	0.07	0.16	0.51	0.47	4.84
1874	0.31	0.44	0.94	0.56	4.22	3.40	0.44	0.64	0.30	0.08	0.57	0.08	12.01
1875	10.45	0.80	0.18	0.84	0.84	1.02	1.48	8.88	0.53	4.18	3.22	2.70	32.88
1876	1.54	2.32	2.88	1.18	2.72	1.88	0.86	0.30	0.45	4.06	4.72	0.64	23.85
1877	2.12	2.01	2.74	1.60	3.16	3.44	2.48	1.24	1.74	1.06	2.82	1.10	35.45
1878	3.72	*2.00	0.75	0.00	2.05	0.22	3.74	0.48	1.35	0.77	1.27	0.80	16.85
1879	1.83	3.11	1.24	1.90	3.00	2.37	1.10	0.51	0.38	1.84	1.03	1.90	20.35
1880	2.08	1.78											
Means	2.34	1.38	1.51	0.93	1.85	1.48	1.20	0.61	0.90	1.11	2.10	1.80	17.22

DAYTON, WASH.

Year.	Jan.	Feb.	Mar.	Apr.	May.	June.	July.	Aug.	Sept.	Oct.	Nov.	Dec.	Annual.
1879												4.55	
1880	3.37	2.19	1.89	3.81	2.78	1.00	1.88	1.29	0.19	1.85	2.00	7.93	29.78
1881	5.03	5.04	1.81	2.51	0.45	1.61	0.65	0.72	1.47	3.04	2.47	2.37	27.70
1882	2.56	8.16	1.97	4.08	1.89	0.77	0.83	0.14	0.94	4.41	2.61	7.12	33.32
1883	5.48	1.17	2.44	1.64	2.90	0.08	0.00	0.30	0.09	1.44	3.11	2.79	21.44
1884	3.14	5.08	1.79	2.40	0.81	2.02	0.32	0.09	1.40	3.45	0.28	5.10	26.43
1885	2.29	3.74	0.05	0.08	3.00	2.30	0.01	0.07	1.15	1.23	2.71		
Means	3.64	3.93	1.66	2.58	1.90	1.26	0.58	0.35	0.87	2.54	2.19	4.98	28.05

EDIZ HOOK LIGHT STATION (PORT ANGELES), WASH.

Year.	Jan.	Feb.	Mar.	Apr.	May.	June.	July.	Aug.	Sept.	Oct.	Nov.	Dec.	Annual.
1881	*8.00	*8.80	*8.00	1.29	1.10	1.40	0.30	0.30	0.35	2.20	4.00	2.40	35.25
1882	*6.00	*6.00	*3.50	*4.50	*1.80	*0.72	*1.40	*1.50	*0.18	*1.94	*3.50	*2.35	36.47
1883	*4.00	*2.90	*1.26	*2.08	*2.00	*0.50		*0.30	*1.90	*3.00	*4.00	4.36	
1884	4.61	4.92	0.42	1.08	0.95	1.75	0.51	1.94	2.90	4.23	1.50	3.53	27.04
1885	8.17	3.01	0.58	0.71	1.47	0.67	0.03	0.00	3.25	2.44	1.80	3.07	28.03
1886	5.54	2.98	3.23	2.07	0.77	0.70	0.46	0.88	1.58	1.86	1.46	7.71	29.96
1887	6.20	4.68	3.05	1.18	2.11	1.12	0.50	0.14	1.18	2.89	4.92	6.07	34.25
1888	8.43	1.58	2.89	1.66	0.21								
Means	5.67	4.25	2.95	2.06	1.29	0.96	0.54	0.72	1.40	2.86	3.55	4.21	30.26

KENNEWICK, WASH.

Year.	Jan.	Feb.	Mar.	Apr.	May.	June.	July.	Aug.	Sept.	Oct.	Nov.	Dec.	Annual.
1884											0.44	0.86	
1885	0.51	0.40	0.04	T.	1.38	0.93	T.	Blk.	0.41	0.20	8.89	1.03	6.04
1886	2.10	0.18	0.27	0.50	0.85	0.30	0.07	T.	0.09	1.17	0.04	2.38	6.76
1887	*2.90	0.67	0.33	0.44	0.35	0.40	0.06	0.24	0.25	0.20	1.38		
Means	1.54	0.45	0.22	0.21	0.50	0.54	0.02	0.12	0.25	0.54	0.71	1.39	6.58

* Interpolated.   † Incomplete, Schott.   T. trace of precipitation.   a Observations at Harney's Depot; latitude 48° 42', longitude 117° 3'.

*Statement showing the precipitation in inches and hundredths—*Continued.

NEAH BAY, WASH.

Year.	Jan.	Feb.	Mar.	Apr.	May.	June.	July.	Aug.	Sept.	Oct.	Nov.	Dec.	Annual.
1863					4.60	7.20	6.10	0.20	11.00	13.20	14.70	27.30	
1864	24.50	10.40	14.80	4.20	1.27	7.10	1.90	2.50	...	3.50	16.00	14.50	109.53
1865	8.36	9.30	16.10	6.50	6.70	5.80	0.30	5.00	13.30	8.44	27.00	14.00	121.30
1866	21.70	10.80	17.00	11.70	0.20	7.50	0.60	2.30	2.50				1126.50
1874	23.85	16.80	5.01	4.00	4.10	4.80	1.30	5.60	4.20	6.80	2.00	9.80	83.05
1875	17.00												
1878										11.50	17.86	8.46	
1879	13.93	24.33	22.93	7.08	7.14	1.48	4.63	5.81	4.90	12.65	8.78	20.97	136.16
1880	25.70	10.70	9.33	3.52	6.62	1.27	2.53	1.08	3.05	5.43	4.88	23.32	97.41
1881	8.76	21.01	12.05	7.02	2.08	4.78	2.31	*2.00	*1.75	*4.50	*4.00	*7.00	70.13
1882													11.83
1883	15.50	8.00	3.60	4.85	6.30	4.40	1.05	4.40	7.20	10.66	6.10	5.00	78.75
1885	17.70	18.50	4.45	8.50	5.70	1.50	0.38	6.05	12.15	7.95	16.50	13.00	161.45
1886	16.40	14.13	12.90	7.55	4.40	3.70	4.60	3.79	5.95	7.40	11.80	30.70	113.23
1887	22.30	7.20	*16.00	*8.00	*7.00	*1.12	*1.24	*1.30	3.80	14.84	*8.00	*20.00	116.89
Means	18.00	13.72	12.28	5.95	5.32	4.23	2.23	2.83	6.35	8.44	12.10	15.83	107.27

NEW TACOMA, WASH.

Year.	Jan.	Feb.	Mar.	Apr.	May.	June.	July.	Aug.	Sept.	Oct.	Nov.	Dec.	Annual.
1884	4.93	*4.00	1.27	*3.40	*1.30	2.81	1.80	1.29	3.21	*4.00	1.78	4.86	34.67
1885	8.30	4.16	1.01	6.47	2.80	0.49	0.26	0.00	2.44	2.47	8.22	6.13	33.74
1886	7.71	2.26	3.36	3.07	1.84	1.93	1.44	0.44	2.12	2.78	1.54	11.00	40.30
1887	5.81	4.08	7.77	3.91	3.42	1.03	0.14	T.	2.35	1.44	4.00	10.20	46.21
Means	5.91	3.63	3.35	2.86	2.36	1.34	0.91	0.43	2.53	2.92	3.88	8.00	38.21

OLYMPIA, WASH.

Year.	Jan.	Feb.	Mar.	Apr.	May.	June.	July.	Aug.	Sept.	Oct.	Nov.	Dec.	Annual.
1877	5.92	14.20	7.90	1.21	1.36	0.24	1.64	6.64	7.00	18.88	11.73		69.34
1878	5.96	15.59	14.44	2.10	*4.72	0.44	2.63	2.11	2.38	6.17	8.49	11.42	73.44
1879	19.00	5.16	5.57	2.47	4.10	1.44	0.52	6.22	1.05	2.63	3.06	16.00	62.77
1880	8.00	16.28	4.03	4.93	1.64	1.93	0.96	0.71	2.47	8.18	6.75	8.86	65.08
1881	6.11	8.60	2.24	4.57	2.39	1.00	0.97	0.81	1.24	6.96	8.77	10.32	51.39
1882	5.68	3.18	2.90	10.78	2.56	0.21	T.	0.01	2.21	3.73	5.10	5.14	41.61
1883	5.47	4.17	1.57	3.60	1.48	3.20	0.60	0.06	3.06	4.30	1.37	5.82	35.58
1884	6.23	7.67	6.26	0.89	2.84	0.79	1.10	0.00	3.60	2.24	16.18	5.72	41.98
1885	8.47	3.79	4.07	4.04	1.90	1.28	1.15	0.43	3.17	4.15	1.73	11.38	46.13
1886	9.83	4.28	10.60	3.04	5.06	1.01	0.74	0.18	3.34	1.51	4.94	15.75	61.78
1888	11.38	2.71	3.96	1.72	0.21								
Means	8.96	7.84	5.44	3.81	2.60	1.15	0.87	0.67	3.10	4.72	6.85	10.17	55.98

PLEASANT GROVE (ELLENSBURGH), WASH.

Year.	Jan.	Feb.	Mar.	Apr.	May.	June.	July.	Aug.	Sept.	Oct.	Nov.	Dec.	Annual.
1884	*3.40	1.98	0.62	1.26	0.17	0.47	1.16	T.	0.33	0.71	0.16	2.97	
1885	0.90	0.44	T.	0.03	1.18	0.57	0.01	T.	0.39	0.06	1.89	1.55	
1886	2.62	0.30	0.24	0.08									
Means	2.31	0.91	0.29	0.76	0.68	0.52	0.59	T.	0.36	0.38	0.92	2.26	9.97

POMEROY, WASH.

Year.	Jan.	Feb.	Mar.	Apr.	May.	June.	July.	Aug.	Sept.	Oct.	Nov.	Dec.	Annual.
1881						1.03	0.57	0.18	1.13	1.90	1.63	2.14	
1882	1.10	2.44	1.05	2.41	1.80	0.27	0.54	0.02	0.51	3.76	1.56	5.46	21.08
1883	3.23	1.09	2.96	1.36	2.37	0.02							
Means	2.21	1.76	2.00	1.88	2.10	0.64	0.66	0.10	0.82	2.86	1.60	3.80	20.33

PORT TOWNSEND, WASH.

Year.	Jan.	Feb.	Mar.	Apr.	May.	June.	July.	Aug.	Sept.	Oct.	Nov.	Dec.	Annual.
1867											1.11	3.60	
1868	1.80	0.55		0.65	0.65	2.62	0.90						
1873	*5.00	*4.00	*3.00	*3.00	*2.00	*1.50	*0.50	0.16	0.40	0.85	1.04	1.05	22.50
1874	2.14	1.24	0.99	1.06	0.87	1.74	0.15	0.33	1.64	0.36	2.08	0.67	13.07
1875	2.34	0.49	3.90	0.12	2.12	2.35	0.00	0.68	0.35	1.84	4.42	2.79	21.50
1876	1.64	1.59	3.86	0.00	1.42	2.10	0.52	0.23	0.79	1.88	1.66	1.88	18.37
1877	2.60	1.58	1.02										
Means	2.62	1.58	2.75	1.15	1.37	2.06	0.23	0.35	0.80	1.23	2.04	2.00	18.18

* Interpolated.   † Incomplete, Schott.   T. trace of precipitation.

Statement showing the precipitation in inches and hundredths—Continued.

PYSHT, WASH.

Year.	Jan.	Feb.	Mar.	Apr.	May.	June.	July.	Aug.	Sept.	Oct.	Nov.	Dec.	Annual.
1883												11.94	
1884	11.20	7.98	1.90	3.17	2.90	2.55	0.73	2.42	4.38	9.53	5.31	5.35	67.51
1885	14.31	12.37	2.07	1.13	2.63	2.17	0.26	0.60	9.44	5.65	13.07	7.98	71.23
1886	11.44	7.81	7.91	4.40	1.81	2.23	1.83	1.50	4.17	4.85	3.54	21.81	73.29
1887	13.76	8.01	a 12.43	*4.50	*6.00	*1.12	*0.90	0.07	*3.80	5.40	*8.00	16.00	80.96
Means	12.70	9.27	6.06	3.32	3.34	2.04	0.92	1.00	5.45	6.43	7.48	12.45	76.49

SAN JUAN ISLAND (CAMP PICKETT OR CAMP STEELE), WASH.

Year.	Jan.	Feb.	Mar.	Apr.	May.	June.	July.	Aug.	Sept.	Oct.	Nov.	Dec.	Annual.
1860		1.36	0.04	0.85	2.05	0.88	0.87	0.62	1.61	1.81	1.55	1.42	
1861	1.26	1.68	6.86	0.97	1.92	0.77	0.07	1.76	0.60	1.45	2.59	4.49	16.11
1862	1.51	1.03	2.60	1.27	2.10	0.48	0.64	0.48	0.86	1.44	0.93	3.74	17.10
1863	2.78	1.06	1.28	0.66	0.46	0.98	0.29	0.23	2.25	2.87	2.40	3.96	19.40
1864	4.92	2.70	1.77	1.19	0.63	0.58	0.80	0.10	1.64	0.84	2.37	2.78	20.41
1865	3.40	0.14	0.84	10.11	1.73							1.20	
1866	2.45	2.43	3.53	1.74					2.00	8.28	4.85	6.80	
1867	3.80	4.50	0.85	2.50	0.26	0.66	1.37	0.26	0.05	3.11	3.70	8.40	36.00
1868	1.65	2.85	2.00	2.12	0.75	3.43	0.07	0.00	0.10	(1)0.57	1.87	4.03	(1)17.04
1869	9.05	1.05	0.28	1.01	1.20	0.00	0.20	0.75	2.10	0.30	8.10	2.80	17.94
1870	2.55	3.19	1.60	0.95	3.23	0.47	0.48	1.10	0.77	2.09	2.50	3.46	19.41
1871	8.96	1.86	1.90	0.65	0.63	0.17	0.42	0.80	3.00	1.28	3.95	5.90	24.39
1872	1.87	3.36	1.84	1.40	6.81	0.06	0.06	8.02	0.63	1.45	*2.00	9.80	22.93
1873	5.38	4.31	7.50	4.50	4.05	25.75	0.49	0.72	*0.40	*0.80	1.28	*1.00	56.09
1874	*5.00	1.28	0.74	0.51	1.33	2.21	*0.20	1.43	5.79		9.21	2.22	29.92
Means	3.12	2.34	1.86	1.40	1.19	2.68	0.45	0.62	1.51	2.05	3.24	4.13	24.40

SEATTLE (2¼ miles north), WASH.

Year.	Jan.	Feb.	Mar.	Apr.	May.	June.	July.	Aug.	Sept.	Oct.	Nov.	Dec.	Annual.
1877	5.96	10.22	5.17	2.15	3.25	3.57	0.56	1.90	4.10	3.25	8.70	4.40	
1878						0.36							
Means	5.96	10.22	5.17	2.15	3.25	1.96	0.55	1.90	4.10	3.25	8.70	4.40	51.03

CAMP SEMIAHMOO, WASH.

Year.	Jan.	Feb.	Mar.	Apr.	May.	June.	July.	Aug.	Sept.	Oct.	Nov.	Dec.	Annual.
1859			8.22	2.12	1.69	2.06	0.63	0.86	3.91	7.88	2.57	0.90	37.85
1860	5.96	2.88	1.98	2.13	2.00	0.75							
Means	5.96	2.88	4.02	2.13	1.84	1.42	0.68	0.80	3.91	7.88	2.57	0.00	33.94

FORT SIMCOE, WASH.

Year.	Jan.	Feb.	Mar.	Apr.	May.	June.	July.	Aug.	Sept.	Oct.	Nov.	Dec.	Annual.
1857				0.00	0.04	0.04	0.11	0.00	0.03	0.32	0.73		
1858	2.11	4.54	1.06	0.40	0.64	0.48	0.03	1.04	0.85	0.83	0.84	0.86	13.78
1859	2.50	1.19	1.39	0.50									
Means	2.30	2.86	1.22	0.33	0.29	0.26	0.07	0.52	0.44	0.56	0.78	0.85	10.60

FORT SPOKANE, WASH.

Year.	Jan.	Feb.	Mar.	Apr.	May.	June.	July.	Aug.	Sept.	Oct.	Nov.	Dec.	Annual.
1883			0.81	0.91	0.56	0.96	0.00	1.00	0.00	1.65	1.14	1.27	
1884	0.62	0.58	0.60	1.11	0.90	1.20	0.66	0.30	1.49	2.34	8.19	0.42	9.51
1885	0.39	1.40	0.00	0.10	1.55	0.89	0.00	0.38	1.14	3.00	2.07	0.44	11.30
1886	1.95	1.41	0.70	1.23	1.26	0.64	0.10	0.00	0.47	1.63	8.54	3.63	13.08
1887	1.43	0.73	1.35	1.82	0.55	2.20	0.27	b 0.65	1.24	0.40	0.64	2.38	13.06
Means	1.05	1.03	0.71	1.03	0.79	1.06	0.21	0.47	0.88	1.78	6.92	1.67	11.00

SPOKANE FALLS, WASH.

Year.	Jan.	Feb.	Mar.	Apr.	May.	June.	July.	Aug.	Sept.	Oct.	Nov.	Dec.	Annual.
1881	*4.50	3.95	1.07	1.20	0.50	1.23	2.25	0.45	2.55	2.41	2.23	2.44	24.68
1882	4.54	2.25	1.01	2.84	1.54	1.17	0.58	0.14	0.80	4.81	2.44	3.54	25.99
1883	2.13	2.95	0.75	1.93	2.11	0.80	0.00	0.15	0.06	1.48	1.98	0.21	14.37
1884	1.79	3.04	1.54	1.33	0.58	2.56	1.06	0.54	2.43	1.82	0.59	3.26	30.58
1885	2.53	3.27	0.72	0.27	1.58	3.40	0.30	0.16	6.86	8.80	4.25	1.81	19.01
1886	3.12	0.61	1.07	1.18	0.92	0.57	0.37	0.33	1.00	2.11	0.71	3.87	15.86
1887	1.91	1.64	2.50	1.88	1.06	2.06	1.41	1.20	1.29	1.04	1.22	2.88	20.10
Means	2.93	2.27	1.24	1.51	1.17	1.68	0.91	0.43	1.29	2.07	1.92	2.58	20.08

* Interpolated.   ‖ Incomplete.   T. trace of precipitation.   a For twenty days.   b Observations for twenty-eight days.

Statement showing the precipitation in inches and hundredths—Continued.

FORT STEILACOOM, WASH.

Year.	Jan.	Feb.	Mar.	Apr.	May.	June.	July.	Aug.	Sept.	Oct.	Nov.	Dec.	Annual.
1849											9.42	8.15	
1850	8.32	4.83	6.70	1.00	0.30	0.40	0.20	0.00	1.20	2.40	5.14	2.62	33.31
1851	15.30	1.47	2.20	3.00	1.05	0.55	0.36	0.81	2.66	3.96	3.02	3.92	39.32
1857	5.51	4.18	4.45	0.26	0.83	1.73	0.10	0.30	2.73	2.07	4.36	13.01	34.58
1858	8.30	3.17	6.70	3.21	3.85	2.65	0.55	4.47	3.80	3.39	4.65	5.34	50.14
1859	6.35	3.42	7.75	0.80	1.40	0.35	0.70	6.44	4.09	4.63	3.37	3.42	34.72
1860	4.85	5.90	2.08	2.36	2.02	0.25	0.86	0.28	1.45	3.14	6.34	4.03	33.56
1861	3.67	4.57	2.77	3.21	1.51	4.03	0.01	1.13	0.86	3.28		5.50	136.67
1862	2.51	1.37	4.47	1.96	2.43	0.98	0.82	1.01	1.12	1.95	0.68	6.26	23.75
1863	6.97	6.18	3.15	2.47	2.20	1.57	1.51	1.20	4.72	3.55	3.45	9.12	45.09
1864	4.40	5.10	4.80	1.50	0.36	1.65	0.34	0.12	2.80	0.99	3.85	6.34	30.65
1865	3.37	2.47	7.02	2.11	1.09	0.84	0.75			6.67	10.53	4.05	137.23
1866	6.06	4.56	7.35	3.02					0.30	3.41	8.26	7.35	
1867	6.52	16.66	7.49	6.74	0.44	1.17		0.23	0.30	3.68	2.80	12.06	158.47
1868	1.36	1.06	4.29										
Means	6.09	4.41	5.08	2.40	1.60	1.42	0.56	0.91	2.18	2.95	4.32	6.51	38.30

NOTE.—Records for 1852, 1853, 1854, 1855 reported as doubtful, and 1856 as incorrect.

FORT STEILACOOM, WASH.

	Jan.	Feb.	Mar.	Apr.	May.	June.	July.	Aug.	Sept.	Oct.	Nov.	Dec.	Annual.
Means	5.60	4.64	4.90	3.32	1.75	1.75	0.47	1.20	2.37	3.26	5.06	6.37	41.29

NOTE.—The above figures represent the monthly averages as deduced from twelve years and four months' observations, from November, 1873, to February, 1886, inclusive.

TATOOSH LIGHT-HOUSE, WASH.

	Jan.	Feb.	Mar.	Apr.	May.	June.	July.	Aug.	Sept.	Oct.	Nov.	Dec.	Annual.
1869					5.74	1.39			3.87	3.30	1.50	20.70	11.75	
1870	10.95	8.70	7.40	3.25	4.49	5.00	0.84	3.40	4.56	3.50	15.42	18.82	84.27
1871	20.50	10.87	15.62	3.62	12.09	1.75	1.00	1.00	6.42	6.62	17.47	15.75	113.01
1872	14.87												
1883										4.36	15.83	16.45	
1884	13.32	5.04	2.41	3.31	4.45	3.06	1.73	5.49	6.15	9.03	6.80	12.47	75.18
1885	14.47	13.29	2.34	0.37	5.46	1.77	0.17	6.33	8.60	7.51	10.25	10.14	84.48
1886	16.82	16.29	10.88	7.04	3.45	3.13	6.32	4.70	5.54	7.81	10.44	25.84	112.47
1887	14.48	11.30	16.36	8.61	8.85	1.12	1.24	1.39	3.43	11.83	18.15	17.47	106.11
Means	15.06	10.08	9.17	4.55	5.74	2.70	1.92	2.82	5.96	6.55	14.51	15.00	93.84

FORT TOWNSEND, WASH.

	Jan.	Feb.	Mar.	Apr.	May.	June.	July.	Aug.	Sept.	Oct.	Nov.	Dec.	Annual.
1860	2.64	1.58										2.33	
1861	2.52	3.00	1.45	1.94	1.58							2.22	
1874								1.48	5.79		9.21	2.22	
1875	1.00	6.02	4.02	2.20	11.31	4.10	0.10	1.18	1.16	3.88	5.72	3.74	38.16
1876	2.49	1.98	4.32	1.04	1.80	2.40	1.04	0.31	0.34	2.10	1.78	1.64	21.83
1877	2.50	1.62	1.46	0.38	1.30	1.34	0.40	0.41	1.38	1.46	2.58	1.44	16.47
1878	3.62	2.42	3.54	1.58	2.10	0.50	0.12	0.12	1.60	1.43	2.94	1.32	21.29
1879	2.54	3.94	2.10	0.56	3.03	0.94	3.92	2.12	0.66	1.16	1.50	1.14	22.71
1880	3.04	0.92	2.16	1.20	2.20	0.92	(1).42	0.54	0.90	1.36	0.80	6.18	21.54
1881	3.20	2.12	1.54	*4.00	0.75	1.61	0.78	1.40	*0.75	1.68	3.98	2.22	24.03
1882	2.76	2.74	2.68	2.89	0.63	1.69	0.82	1.06	0.16	1.84	3.72	3.35	24.20
1883	3.97	1.93	1.26	2.98	0.85	0.32	0.60	0.36	0.55	2.47	3.91	2.34	20.18
1884	2.96	1.77	0.11	2.11	0.97	2.23	0.86	2.02	2.04	2.14	0.30	1.57	18.57
1885	2.44	2.00	0.30	0.68	3.40	0.87	0.09	0.00	2.10	1.00	*3.50	1.70	18.14
1886	2.86	0.37	0.54	1.62	0.76	0.24	0.37	0.23	0.87	2.61	1.22	5.10	15.85
1887	3.30	1.19	1.75	0.90	1.66	1.29	0.12	0.15	0.85	1.47	2.00	3.45	16.73
Means	2.62	1.83	1.95	1.77	2.31	1.41	0.75	0.82	1.38	1.71	3.03	2.65	22.43

FORT VANCOUVER, WASH.

	Jan.	Feb.	Mar.	Apr.	May.	June.	July.	Aug.	Sept.	Oct.	Nov.	Dec.	Annual.
1849												6.00	
1850	6.66	2.60	6.71	0.80	0.40	3.72	3.35	0.00	0.89	2.00	4.90	1.29	38.40
1851	9.55	2.94	4.08									7.48	
1852	9.31	4.77	4.26	6.56	3.40	1.77		0.39	2.00	1.55	7.37	19.37	155.95
1853	9.30	4.23	2.47	1.72	2.33	0.90	0.90		0.39	3.68	11.57	3.22	42.07

* Interpolated. | Incomplete, Schott.   T. trace of precipitation.

Statement showing the precipitation in inches and hundredths—Continued.

FORT VANCOUVER, WASH.—Continued.

Year.	Jan.	Feb.	Mar.	Apr.	May.	June.	July.	Aug.	Sept.	Oct.	Nov.	Dec.	Annual.
1854	......	2.83	1.72	2.76	0.75	2.11	0.00	1.72	0.00	2.31	3.19	8.34	192.75
1855	13.29	3.84	3.20	2.04	3.77	2.43	......	0.00	0.46	1.41	2.05	10.77	145.43
1856	5.00	3.07	1.01	4.01	4.08	3.26	2.80	0.68	2.37	4.81	6.62	15.37	82.57
1857	6.74	4.98	7.30	4.37	3.04	3.09	......	0.14	1.87	6.96	7.01	13.28	147.57
1858	5.82	6.90	4.24	1.84	7.30	1.82	0.00	0.71	4.37	3.56	4.25	4.76	40.46
1859	5.77	5.10	9.60	1.90	2.00	0.16	0.25	1.02	4.49	2.23	4.15	2.40	38.86
1860	5.57	2.77	2.03	1.05	2.62	1.00	1.25	0.35	1.52	3.74	6.31	4.12	34.47
1861	4.50	0.92	3.05	3.05	3.40	2.70	0.00	0.20	0.75	2.66	7.78	7.40	42.06
1862	3.47	1.81	5.31	3.04	3.87	3.05	1.43	1.00	0.45	1.30	0.85	4.87	30.40
1863	8.70	6.48	3.75	2.50	2.45	0.90	1.10	0.85	1.70	3.61	4.23	5.36	42.41
1864	5.35	1.73	3.94	1.90	0.67	1.79	0.34	0.30	2.81	1.06	5.93	5.67	31.48
1865	2.38	11.32	2.71	11½.	0.78	0.94	0.83	0.88	......	0.68	6.63	1.85	†25.91
1866	6.40	0.99	4.15	2.11	......	......	......	......	0.08	1.53	2.63	4.69	......
1867	3.85	3.66	0.97	1.08	0.90	0.79	1.19	0.00	1.14	2.45	7.14	16.94	35.19
1868	2.23	1.02	2.89	2.36	1.01	3.78	0.55	......	......	......	......	......	......
Means	6.01	3.40	3.87	2.47	2.24	1.94	1.32	0.48	1.50	2.58	5.14	7.18	36.03

WALLA WALLA, WASH.

Year	Jan.	Feb.	Mar.	Apr.	May.	June.	July.	Aug.	Sept.	Oct.	Nov.	Dec.	Annual.
1869	......	......	......	......	......	......	......	......	......	......	......	5.88	......
1870	4.41	......	......	......	......	......	......	......	......	......	......	......	......
1877	......	1.62	4.17	0.58	5.20	0.96	1.28	0.10	1.40	1.18	2.72	0.79	......
1878	a1.29	a2.24	a1.59	a0.16	a2.17	......	a0.67	a0.99	a1.25	......	......	......	......
1879	......	......	......	......	......	......	......	......	1.62	0.29	1.83	......	......
1885	......	......	......	......	......	......	......	......	......	......	......	1.92	......
1886	3.43	1.29	1.90	1.66	0.67	0.72	0.12	0.66	1.96	0.78	4.41	16.20	
1887	2.36	1.78	1.83	1.57	1.04	2.12	0.03	0.71	1.55	1.92	3.06	2.83	20.44
Means	2.86	1.73	2.15	0.99	2.28	1.27	0.50	0.39	1.18	1.24	2.10	3.11	19.66

FORT WALLA WALLA, WASH.

Year	Jan.	Feb.	Mar.	Apr.	May.	June.	July.	Aug.	Sept.	Oct.	Nov.	Dec.	Annual.
1857	0.91	1.44	1.47	0.28	3.42	1.40	1.28	0.00	1.22	0.64	2.68	3.15	17.89
1858	1.96	2.62	2.76	2.03	1.92	1.72	0.26	0.90	1.30	1.64	1.95	1.36	19.12
1859	0.50	1.82	3.90	2.38	2.22	0.04	0.14	0.28	3.33	0.60	2.40	0.72	18.19
1860	4.84	1.92	0.79	0.2.	2.36	1.54	2.44	0.66	0.36	2.44	4.52	2.84	20.50
1861	4.84	4.23	2.28	1.06	4.37	6.92	0.02	0.00	0.50	2.36	6.94	12.84	40.97
1862	11.03	10.80	......	1.96	5.76	2.78	*0.10	......	4.31	0.05	0.00	0.04	196.27
1863	0.06	0.11	......	0.11	0.08	0.00	0.00	0.02	1.33	0.36	0.37	1.30	15.29
1864	0.80	0.90	0.15	0.20	0.70	1.00	0.09	0.00	0.40	0.33	2.13	0.41	16.38
1865	0.55	0.34	0.55	0.24	0.44	0.30	0.13	......	......	0.36	(†)0.30	......	......
1866	......	......	......	......	......	......	......	......	......	......	......	1.92	......
1867	3.08	0.70	0.10	0.22	1.45	......	......	......	......	......	......	......	......
1875	0.50	0.78	1.07	3.08	1.82	0.95	0.44	0.85	0.51	4.44	3.87	0.84	19.10
1877	1.21	1.87	4.44	0.90	5.40	0.53	1.07	0.12	1.42	1.26	2.61	0.57	21.20
1878	1.16	1.40	1.34	*0.16	1.96	*0.02	0.25	0.19	*1.00	*0.50	*0.72	*0.36	9.09
1879	0.72	1.83	*1.26	*1.49	*1.06	*0.80	*0.20	*0.03	*1.00	*0.33	*0.40	*1.82	10.87
1880	*3.45	*1.20	T.	0.62	0.48	0.56	0.02	0.16	0.09	1.84	0.37	7.86	17.28
1887	0.50	1.95	2.17	1.08	0.68	1.58	0.09	0.32	0.57	0.61	1.02	1.44	11.95
Means	2.04	2.09	1.59	1.08	2.15	0.95	0.43	0.27	1.17	1.24	1.88	2.40	17.29

HELENA, MONT.

Year	Jan.	Feb.	Mar.	Apr.	May.	June.	July.	Aug.	Sept.	Oct.	Nov.	Dec.	Annual.
1880	......	......	......	2.22	1.24	0.46	0.98	1.28	0.00	1.27	0.87	4.64	......
1881	2.88	0.51	0.00	1.65	1.00	3.51	1.85	1.78	2.40	2.04	1.27	0.38	19.94
1882	1.04	0.37	0.31	0.94	0.54	1.18	6.26	0.15	3.66	1.10	0.15	0.48	10.92
1883	0.67	0.73	0.73	0.53	1.54	1.74	0.22	......	......	......	0.86	1.02	......
1884	3.75	1.33	0.60	1.06	0.69	4.79	3.25	0.47	1.30	0.49	0.46	1.86	19.18
1885	1.31	0.82	0.28	1.00	0.85	4.16	1.16	0.44	0.11	0.16	0.15	0.21	10.90
1886	0.82	0.56	0.00	2.89	0.49	1.14	0.65	0.08	2.40	1.57	0.49	0.99	12.63
1887	1.35	0.61	0.12	1.03	2.41	3.48	0.27	1.96	0.50	1.04	0.22	0.29	14.05
1888	0.79	0.12	1.32	0.52	2.90	......	......	......	......	......	......	......	......
Means	1.56	0.63	0.54	1.39	1.35	2.50	1.09	0.88	1.49	1.06	0.13	1.20	14.27

*Interpolated.
†Incomplete, Schott.

a Observations at latitude 46° 3′; longitude 117° 53′ 45″, altitude 870 feet.
T. trace of precipitation.

APPENDIX No. 3.

Monthly percentage of rain-fall at stations in Washington Territory and Oregon.

[The annual rain-fall is represented by 100 per cent.]

WASHINGTON TERRITORY.

Stations.	Jan.	Feb.	Mar.	Apr.	May.	June.	July.	Aug.	Sept.	Oct.	Nov.	Dec.
Tatoosh Island	16	11	16	5	6	3	2	3	6	7	17	16
Neah Bay	17	13	11	6	3	4	2	3	6	8	11	15
Fort Canby	15	13	12	7	4	3	3	1	4	8	14	16
San Juan Island	13	9	8	6	5	11	2	3	6	8	13	15
Ediz Hook Light	19	14	10	7	4	3	2	2	5	8	12	14
Port Townsend	14	9	16	6	8	11	1	2	4	7	11	11
Port Blakely	14	13	11	7	8	3	2	2	5	8	11	18
Olympia	16	14	10	6	5	2	2	1	6	8	12	18
Cathlamet	16	10	19	9	5	4	1	2	2	7	13	14
Fort Vancouver	16	9	16	7	6	5	3	1	4	6	13	19
Pleasant Grove*	23	9	3	8	7	5	6	6	4	4	9	23
Fort Simcoe*	22	27	11	3	3	2	1	5	4	5	7	9
Fort Colville	14	9	9	5	10	9	7	4	4	7	12	16
Fort Spokane	9	9	6	9	7	9	2	3	7	10	8	15
Spokane Falls	16	12	6	8	6	8	5	2	8	10	16	13
Dayton	14	15	6	10	7	5	2	1	3	10	8	19
Fort Walla Walla	14	9	11	5	11	6	3	1	6	7	11	16
Helena, Mont	11	4	4	9	9	18	9	6	10	9	4	8

OREGON.

Stations.	Jan.	Feb.	Mar.	Apr.	May.	June.	July.	Aug.	Sept.	Oct.	Nov.	Dec.
Astoria	17	11	13	7	5	4	2	2	4	6	13	16
Fort Stevens	14	13	13	6	4	4	2	2	4	9	14	14
Fort Yamhill	17	13	14	5	4	3	1	1	5	5	14	18
Fort Hoskins	19	14	13	7	4	3	1	1	5	8	13	17
Empire City	16	18	8	7	4	3	1	1	3	8	16	19
Bandon	18	15	16	8	6	2	1	1	3	7	9	16
Portland	15	14	13	7	5	3	1	1	4	6	13	17
Zola	15	16	13	7	5	3	1	1	4	7	16	15
Albany	18	14	9	8	6	3	1	1	5	7	9	19
Block House	12	12	16	6	6	2	1	1	8	8	14	13
Roseburgh	18	13	9	8	5	3	2	1	8	8	11	19
Ashland	15	11	6	16	8	5	3	9	4	8	11	20
The Dalles	18	14	9	5	4	3	1	1	3	9	12	20
Fort Klamath	16	13	13	6	5	3	2	1	3	7	14	17
Linkville ?	16	11	9	11	8	9	4	1	2	6	8	14
Camp Watson‡	12	6	16	10	9	15	1	0	5	2	8	24
Camp Warner	11	14	8	8	13	4	2	1	4	2	12	20
Lakeview	18	11	9	9	7	16	2	2	5	5	9	12
Umatilla	14	12	9	8	6	4	3	4	8	9	9	14
Camp Harney	14	16	12	9	8	7	3	2	2	4	13	15
Boise City, Idaho	16	11	6	14	8	7	1	1	3	9	5	15

* Two years' record.   ‡ One year's record.

APPENDIX No. 4.

Temperature data for Oregon.

Name of station.	County.	Latitude.	Longitude.	Elevation.	Record. Length	Record. From—	Record. To (inclusive)—	Remarks as to observers and character of records.
		o ′	o ′	Feet.	Yrs. Mos.			
Albany (near)	Linn	44 35	122 50	800	9 0	Jan., 1867	Dec., 1887	Jan., 1867, to Jan., 1858, S. M. Hindman. Jan., 1879, to Dec., 1887, John Briggs.
Ashland	Jackson	42 12	122 38	1,910	4 0	Jan., 1884	Dec., 1847	Signal Service.
Astoria	Clatsop	46 11	123 49	50	27 2	Aug., 1850	May, 1886	Aug., 1856, to Dec., 1851, United States post hospital; observations at sunrise, 9 a. m., 3 p. m., and 9 p. m. Jan., 1855, to Dec., 1876 L. Wilson, U. S. Coast Survey; observations at 8 a. m., noon, and 6 p.m. Jan., 1867, to May, 1886, Signal Service.
Bandon	Coos	43 07	124 24	55	8 0	Jan., 1880	Dec., 1887	Geo. Bennett.
Black House	Benton	44 25	122 30		5 0	Jan., 1858	Dec., 1862	United States post hospital.
Dalles, Fort	Columbia	45 36	120 55	350	13 4	Sept., 1850	Mar., 1860	United States post hospital; observations at sunrise, 9 a. m., 3 and 9 p.m.
East Portland	Multnomah	45 31	122 27	30	4 0	Jan., 1841	Dec., 1887	George Wigg, M. D.
Eola	Polk	44 57	122 54	500	18 0	Jan., 1870	Dec., 1887	T. Pearce.
Harney, Camp	Grant	43 00	119 00	4,060	11 6	Dec., 1867	May, 1880	United States post hospital.
Hopkins, Fort	Polk	45 02	123 22		8 4	Nov., 1840	Mar., 1865	Do.
Klamath, Fort	Klamath	42 40	121 54	4,200	17 9	Dec., 1863	Dec., 1887	Dec., 1863, to Mar., 1865, United States post hospital. Jan., 1871, to Dec., 1887, Signal Service.
La Grande	Union	45 20	118 7	2,600	1 6	July, 1886	Dec., 1887	J. K. Renaig. Observations from maximum and minimum thermometers.
Lakeview	Lake	40 12	120 12	4,830	4 0	Jan., 1884	Dec., 1887	Signal service.
Linkville	Klamath	42 14	120 40	4,160	4 0	Jan., 1884	Dec., 1887	Do.
Mount Angel	Marion	45 33	122 05	150	1 5	June, 1886	Oct., 1887	F. Barnabas Held. Observations at 7 a.m. and afternoon.
Newport	Benton	44 42	134 02		3 0	Jan., 1830	Dec., 1887	Dr. J. G. Jessup.
Oregon City	Clackamas	45 20	122 24	200	3 0	Jan., 1819	Dec., 1851	Rev. G. M. Atkinson. Observations at sunrise, 2 p. m., and sunset.
Portland	Multnomah	45 24	122 30	150	19 5	Apr., 1858	May, 1888	Apr., 1858, to Aug., 1850, G. H. Stebbins; observations at 6 a.m., noon, and 6 p. m. Jan., 1879, to Dec., 1871, J. S. Reed, S. W. Gilliland, H. A. Oxer. Jan., 1872, to May, 1888, Signal Service.
Orford, Port	Curry	42 44	124 20	50	4 0	June, 1852	June, 1876	June, 1852, to July, 1858, United States post hospital; observations at sunrise, 9 a. m., 3 p. m., 9 p.m. July, 1875, to June, 1876, F. Unican.
Roseburgh	Douglas	43 16	123 20	523	10 11	July, 1877	May, 1888	Signal Service.
Salem	Marion	44 56	172 45	120	1 1	Oct., 1856	Oct., 1883	Oct., 1856, to Sept., 1857, Patent Office and Smithsonian reports. Oct., 1863, P. L. Willis.
Stevens, Fort	Clatsop	46 12	123 57		15 2	Nov., 1865	May, 1883	United States post hospital.
The Dalles	Wasco	45 36	121 12	116	13 0	Jan., 1875	Dec., 1887	Do.
Three Forks, Camp	Owyhee	42 15	116 54		2 0	Jan., 1868	Dec., 1869	United States post hospital.
Umatilla	Umatilla	45 58	110 22	290	5 9	July, 1877	Mar., 1883	Signal Service.
Umpqua, Fort	Douglas	43 42	124 10	8	5 10	Aug., 1856	May, 1862	United States post hospital.
Warner, Camp	Lake	42 50	120 0		6 8	Jan., 1868	Aug., 1874	Do.
Watson, Camp	Grant	44 13	119 45		2 4	Jan., 1867	Apr., 1860	Do.
Yamhill, Fort	Yamhill	45 21	123 30		9 7	Oct., 1856	Apr., 1866	Do.
Boisé City, Idaho	Ada	43 37	116 8	2,750	10 10	July, 1877	May, 1884	Signal Service.

NOTE.—Where not otherwise mentioned observations were taken at 7 a. m., 2 p. m., and 9 p.m.

Statement showing mean temperatures.

NEAR ALBANY, OREGON.

Year.	Jan.	Feb.	Mar.	Apr.	May.	June.	July.	Aug.	Sept.	Oct.	Nov.	Dec.	Annual.
1867	41.3	39.5	37.9	52.3	58.6		87.8	72.1	62.7				
1868	22.8												
1870	*37.6	*30.9	*46.1	51.0	53.8	59.8	64.7	66.2	61.8	50.0	41.5	39.8	51.0
1880	41.3	36.6	40.4	49.5	53.4	59.1	66.0	63.2	59.0	50.5	40.7	41.5	50.0
1841	40.5	40.5	48.4	54.5	56.1	59.5	63.2	62.5	58.4	48.7	41.5	42.4	51.8
1842	a35.2	37.5	43.7	48.4	56.8	63.2	64.1	64.7	59.6	49.9	41.7	44.4	50.8
1843	34.4	35.3	50.3	48.9	57.4	64.0	64.5	63.8	60.4	*51.5	40.4	36.0	61.4
1844	36.9	37.0	45.0	52.7	56.7	61.5	63.3	64.2	53.3	52.5	47.4	22.1	51.0
1865	39.4	47.8	53.1	51.4	80.3	60.9	68.4	67.6	62.8	58.3	47.3	44.6	51.9
1846	38.8	48.5	46.4	52.1	56.9	63.6	68.9	68.5	63.9	51.3	43.2	40.5	54.3
1847	43.8	22.7	49.7	51.0	56.7	61.5	65.0	65.0	80.2	52.8	43.8	42.2	52.3
Means	37.6	39.9	46.1	51.2	57.3	61.5	66.0	66.1	80.2	51.5	43.7	41.6	51.9

ASHLAND, OREGON.

Year.	Jan.	Feb.	Mar.	Apr.	May.	June.	July.	Aug.	Sept.	Oct.	Nov.	Dec.	Annual.
1884	40.8	38.6	45.4	46.2	69.8	74.4	75.4	73.4	58.0	50.4	44.6	37.0	54.5
1885	40.9	48.2	52.4	54.4	58.8	69.7	71.6	69.3	61.9	57.2	46.8	42.6	55.3
1886	38.8	46.2	43.7	49.1	58.8	64.6	68.7	69.3	63.1	50.7	40.8	43.0	53.2
1887	40.0	33.0	40.3	49.0	57.8	61.7	68.8	68.5	61.6	58.0	43.8	*40.8	52.3
Means	40.1	41.0	47.7	49.7	61.6	65.4	71.4	69.8	61.1	53.5	44.0	40.9	53.8

ASTORIA, OREGON.

Year.	Jan.	Feb.	Mar.	Apr.	May.	June.	July.	Aug.	Sept.	Oct.	Nov.	Dec.	Annual.
1850								62.3	50.4	55.4	46.4	46.7	
1851	43.0	48.5	45.7	52.8	55.0	58.5	61.6	53.8	56.1	*52.2	*45.8	*40.7	51.8
1853	32.3								59.4		46.5	43.6	
1854	32.8	39.6	*44.1	49.5	51.8	55.1	59.2	60.4	58.2	53.5	40.9	43.0	46.7
1855	*38.2	44.8	49.2	48.6	52.2	57.7	61.8	62.0	59.2	55.2	45.0	35.8	50.4
1856	42.4	41.2	48.9	50.4	53.5	67.1	58.7	59.1	58.8	56.0	*46.2	39.9	50.8
1857	39.7	43.1	48.0	52.6	56.1	58.4	60.0	58.7	58.2	54.3	46.1	44.0	51.4
1858	40.9	41.4	41.0	47.6	53.1	58.1	58.6	60.7	58.2	50.6	47.6	39.0	50.0
1859	40.1	46.9	41.4	48.2	52.4	56.2	58.6	59.9	58.0	53.6	41.9	37.4	48.3
1860	41.5	43.8	45.8	47.2	51.8	56.4	58.6	63.4	59.4	53.4	45.8	43.8	50.3
1861	41.8	43.4	44.8	47.3	56.4	55.3	59.7	60.5	59.3	51.4	43.1	40.5	49.3
1862	38.2	34.6	42.0	48.4	53.3	56.2	60.9	60.0	57.2	52.3	44.6	41.2	48.4
1863	41.1	39.1	44.5	48.7	52.5	57.0	62.1	58.8	58.1	51.0	44.8	42.9	49.9
1864	36.0	44.6	45.8	49.4	54.3	75.7	58.8	60.5	57.3	52.8	45.2	36.0	50.2
1865	38.0	28.1	39.3	46.1	53.9	56.5	58.8	58.8	56.1	52.7	48.8	35.0	48.5
1866	39.0	38.7	44.3	47.0	51.9	55.5	60.3	56.8	57.8	52.7	48.8	44.1	45.7
1867	40.7	39.4	37.4	47.5	53.2	58.9	60.9	61.3	57.0	50.9	47.3	42.6	49.7
1868	29.7	38.5	42.9	49.5	53.6	53.6	60.5	56.2	54.7	52.3	45.7	44.3	49.0
1869	41.7	41.6	48.2	50.8	55.8	59.4	59.6	56.1	57.4	52.3	48.0	42.3	51.2
1870	41.2	42.4	41.1	48.5	52.3	57.4	64.2	63.8	58.0	52.3	47.5	36.8	50.5
1871	43.0	40.3	44.3	47.1	49.7	56.1	58.4	60.0	60.0	51.6	44.5	30.1	49.3
1872	40.1	44.3	47.1	48.5	52.0	56.3	59.8	50.2	57.0	52.4	42.9	41.9	50.0
1873	43.7	38.9	48.2	49.0	51.9	55.4	60.1	61.5	58.2	56.4	57.4	37.7	50.9
1874	40.4	40.1	41.5	48.9	53.4	55.3	58.8	58.8	59.0	54.0	45.2	42.1	49.8
1875	32.2	40.1	41.8	48.1	50.0	55.4	59.4	50.7	58.2	56.8	43.9	46.1	49.2
1876	37.4	42.6	42.6	47.3	50.3	57.3	58.3	58.0	58.6	*53.1	*46.2	*41.0	49.4
1887	*34.5	*41.2	48.3	47.2	53.5	56.0	58.5	50.3	50.9	53.1	45.9	43.1	49.9
1888	34.7	42.8	45.3	50.8	58.4								
Means	38.5	41.2	44.2	48.5	52.6	57.0	59.9	60.3	57.9	63.7	46.3	41.0	50.0

BANDON, OREGON.

Year.	Jan.	Feb.	Mar.	Apr.	May.	June.	July.	Aug.	Sept.	Oct.	Nov.	Dec.	Annual.
1880	45.2	42.0	43.6	47.5	52.0	55.5	59.4	58.9	55.4	53.8	47.6	49.8	50.6
1881	48.2	51.4	49.6	54.8	54.3	57.4	59.2	60.9	57.7	52.3	47.9	48.3	53.3
1882	43.7	42.5	44.5	47.6	52.2	57.3	57.1	59.2	58.2	53.4	48.0	49.1	51.0
1883	44.5	40.9	49.4	47.9	49.0	53.9	52.8	54.9	55.9	50.7	47.2	44.9	49.4
1884	43.8	40.1	45.7	49.4	52.7	55.5	58.1	58.0	54.4	51.0	50.1	43.6	50.5
1885	46.3	47.5	48.8	50.7	54.3	54.8	58.8	53.5	54.4	56.0	47.7	45.8	48.9
1886	42.4	48.6	41.5	45.0	49.7	55.0	56.8	54.1	51.3	47.0	43.3	48.4	48.2
1887	43.6	38.0	47.9	48.8	53.0	54.1	54.6	56.1	51.6	66.5	47.6	*47.1	48.3
Means	44.7	43.4	46.4	49.0	52.3	55.5	56.7	57.6	54.9	60.9	47.4	47.1	50.4

BLOCK HOUSE, OREGON.

Year.	Jan.	Feb.	Mar.	Apr.	May.	June.	July.	Aug.	Sept.	Oct.	Nov.	Dec.	Annual.
1858	*43.4	*45.1	45.4	48.8	53.8	59.0	50.8	60.8	59.2	49.4	49.1	39.8	51.1
1859	41.3	41.8	41.3	47.2	52.0	60.4	*58.8	61.1	57.2	52.7	42.4	40.3	48.7
1860	43.3	44.8	44.0	46.8	52.4	58.7	60.7	63.2	56.3	53.4	47.6	*40.5	51.1
1861	*39.4	45.4	*43.4	*47.1	50.0	*58.6	61.2	61.8	63.0	54.9	*44.9	42.0	51.0
1862	29.7	37.3	43.1	44.5	52.3	58.2	62.5	72.4	56.9	50.6	46.6	40.8	48.2
Means	39.4	42.8	43.4	46.9	52.1	58.6	60.6	61.9	59.0	52.2	44.9	40.5	50.2

*Interpolated.   a Last fifteen days of month.

Statement showing mean temperatures—Continued.

FORT DALLES, OREGON.

Year.	Jan.	Feb.	Mar.	Apr.	May.	June.	July.	Aug.	Sept.	Oct.	Nov.	Dec.	Annual.
1850									57.4	52.6	37.9	32.6	
1851	38.0	41.4	46.7										
1852										58.8	41.2	38.0	
1853	32.3	37.1	48.8	52.4	62.1	60.6	74.9	70.2	58.7	55.4	41.8	46.1	53.4
1854	32.6	38.9	46.0	58.5	58.9	63.5	71.5	71.3	64.0	52.9	44.3	37.1	52.0
1855	46.2	42.6	49.3	52.0	57.7	71.2	*73.2	76.9	64.6	61.5	46.4	39.5	55.4
1856		42.3	50.9									32.3	
1857	39.6	42.1	49.5	56.8	63.1	66.3	72.1	71.5	63.2	52.9	42.3	41.1	54.1
1858	36.8	38.3	48.5	54.3	60.2	67.9	71.6	72.6	65.3	49.9	42.8	33.9	53.3
1859	39.4	36.7	41.7	52.3	66.2	70.1	73.6	70.6	63.4	53.2	36.8	23.2	51.3
1860	33.4	40.5	45.7	51.6	58.0	68.4	72.9	75.5	65.4	54.9	47.2	38.0	54.3
1861	37.0	44.2	47.8	53.2	57.8	65.0	74.6	71.3	67.3	52.8	42.6	33.8	54.0
1862	30.0	32.0	40.1	52.1	60.8	67.0	71.2	74.4	64.0	56.7	38.8	35.6	49.7
1863	37.3	38.6	47.7	54.5	62.8	70.8	78.4	78.5	66.1	53.1	44.7	38.7	55.0
1864	34.4	45.0	*46.4	56.1	68.5	57.4	74.7	73.2	62.9	53.9	42.5	32.7	54.0
1865	29.6	33.6	46.3	51.4	64.2	68.6	74.0	73.2	60.7	57.3	47.0	28.4	52.4
1866	28.2	30.3	45.6										
Means	31.5	38.1	45.9	53.4	61.2	67.1	73.7	72.5	62.8	54.3	42.4	38.6	53.1

EAST PORTLAND, OREGON.

Year	Jan.	Feb.	Mar.	Apr.	May.	June.	July.	Aug.	Sept.	Oct.	Nov.	Dec.	Annual.
1884	*39.2	*39.1	41.0	52.7	57.2	61.7	61.9	69.5	53.5	50.4	43.4	27.3	49.7
1885	34.0	40.4	48.6	47.8	56.3	58.8	66.7	62.2	56.6	53.5	44.8	41.2	51.3
1886	42.0	42.6	47.0	54.0	52.0	71.5	70.0	63.0	64.0	53.5	41.0	44.0	55.3
1887	38.5	34.0	56.1	60.0	61.5	68.0	66.0	65.0	64.4	51.0	40.0	41.0	52.8
Means	39.2	39.1	47.9	50.9	58.2	65.2	66.2	66.4	60.5	52.1	42.2	38.4	52.3

EOLA, OREGON.

Year	Jan.	Feb.	Mar.	Apr.	May.	June.	July.	Aug.	Sept.	Oct.	Nov.	Dec.	Annual.
1870	36.4	39.0	39.4	46.8	51.0	58.5	67.4	68.6	58.2	40.3	42.1	23.2	48.2
1871	40.2	37.1	41.5	46.0	48.8	60.0	82.8	57.0	64.0	48.4	41.0	34.8	48.8
1872	34.5	41.0	46.3	43.2	52.8	60.3	74.0	62.6	58.1	50.4	37.6	38.4	49.1
1873	39.8	35.3	43.7	46.6	51.1	54.5	61.7	62.2	57.1	45.4	42.6	*38.5	48.3
1874	42.7	42.7	46.7	53.8	58.9	66.4	67.6	65.1	63.4	56.7	45.0	41.6	53.7
1875	36.0	30.3	41.0	54.0	53.3	59.3	65.9	67.6	62.0	56.4	40.0	44.9	51.7
1876	35.7	41.5	41.9	47.3	52.8	60.0	62.3	64.9	65.3	50.7	41.8	35.8	50.7
1877	39.6	44.3	49.2	50.7	53.1	59.8	63.8	65.0	58.1	52.1	45.7	40.7	51.9
1878	49.7	14.6	51.3	49.6	54.6	62.2	65.5	65.4	58.6	49.3	45.6	37.1	51.9
1879	35.1	42.1	41.3	51.4	52.0	58.2	62.8	66.3	61.5	49.7	60.4	37.2	45.9
1880	39.8	35.8	38.8	48.1	48.2	57.8	65.1	62.9	59.7	51.5	40.5	40.9	44.8
1881	39.2	*39.3	47.0	53.3	53.0	58.4	61.4	61.2	57.2	47.4	40.8	42.2	50.1
1882	36.0	37.0	46.9	46.5	53.4	61.0	63.9	63.2	58.2	46.7	41.3	43.2	49.6
1883	36.0	33.1	49.7	47.5	58.8	62.3	66.6	63.8	61.6	48.7	45.9	40.3	51.0
1884	36.9	34.3	54.1	51.5	57.8	60.0	61.6	67.2	52.3	51.4	44.7	30.7	56.2
1885	36.1	45.5	52.4	52.3	56.6	59.3	66.0	66.2	61.0	55.6	45.8	43.9	53.0
1886	36.3	43.4	42.8	48.8	58.0	61.5	67.4	65.7	53.2	56.0	41.1	47.0	51.9
1887	41.0	31.0	46.2	47.4	55.8	58.1	63.6	62.9	58.3	*51.3	43.2	40.2	49.9
Means	37.5	39.3	45.3	49.2	53.5	59.6	64.7	64.8	59.6	51.3	42.6	39.5	50.6

CAMP HARNEY, OREGON.

Year	Jan.	Feb.	Mar.	Apr.	May.	June.	July.	Aug.	Sept.	Oct.	Nov.	Dec.	Annual.
1867											23.3		
1868	11.8	19.6	36.5	46.3	52.4	60.7	76.7	70.8	62.9	52.2	30.0	35.3	46.3
1869	29.3	36.7	41.3	49.6	62.0	73.1	74.9	68.8	60.0	50.8	41.6	28.9	51.0
1870	27.1	35.0	33.8	49.8	56.4	68.2	77.2	72.3	64.1	50.5	46.6	24.6	50.0
1871	33.6	33.3	27.6	45.6	53.3	70.4	77.7	73.9	65.8	49.6	36.9	33.6	50.8
1872	27.8	35.3	38.1	52.7	58.7	67.4	77.6	67.6	51.9	48.9	27.0	28.7	47.7
1873	35.4	34.5	37.8	49.4	49.5	58.4	70.0	66.9	58.7	44.7	60.4	22.9	45.6
1874											35.2	26.0	
1875	11.8	25.3	30.5	47.5	52.0	56.8	73.0	67.9	62.1	52.7	31.9	31.5	45.8
1876	21.6	29.3	31.1	43.0	50.3	64.3	67.3	62.5	56.3	34.9	24.4	45.3	
1877	20.2	32.4	40.6	42.5	46.7	58.6	66.0	67.3	56.1	43.5	34.7	27.9	45.5
1878	27.5	30.7	40.2	43.5	50.4	63.9	65.1	66.4	55.1	42.5	37.1	25.8	45.9
1879	20.9	21.0	38.1	44.8	44.6	57.3	67.5	60.9	62.0	43.9	30.4	22.7	44.6
1880	26.7	22.7	26.4	30.3	43.0								
Means	25.0	29.1	36.3	44.5	51.8	63.9	71.2	66.9	60.1	48.1	35.9	28.7	47.0

FORT HOSKINS, OREGON.

Year	Jan.	Feb.	Mar.	Apr.	May.	June.	July.	Aug.	Sept.	Oct.	Nov.	Dec.	Annual.
1856											42.1	38.5	
1857	38.6	42.4	46.9	56.6	58.3	62.3	64.1	64.2	60.6	53.5	44.5	43.0	52.9
1858	40.1	42.4	46.2	52.9	56.5	68.4	64.4	66.7	61.8	48.4	47.7	37.9	52.3
1859	36.6	40.5	40.3	48.8	54.3	64.1	62.8	63.3	57.6	53.6	46.5	36.1	50.1
1860	41.1	44.3	48.1	48.7	52.8	50.3	62.0	66.8	60.1	53.3	48.6	40.9	52.0

*Interpolated.

*Statement showing mean temperatures—*Continued.

FORT HOSKINS, OREGON—Continued.

Year.	Jan.	Feb.	Mar.	Apr.	May.	June.	July.	Aug.	Sept.	Oct.	Nov.	Dec.	Annual.
1861	*42.2	43.0	46.8	49.5	51.6	56.8	64.6	61.9	60.4	50.2	46.1	40.9	51.2
1862	36.8	35.4	42.2	48.0	51.4	59.7	61.7	61.5	58.9	56.0	40.5	41.4	49.4
1863	41.4	40.2	45.3	48.7	54.7	50.8	60.1	62.5	60.0	52.0	44.5	44.5	51.0
1864	40.2	46.4	47.8	51.0	57.8	57.9	62.8	63.8	59.3	*52.3	*45.1	*40.4	52.1
1865		36.0	42.9										
Means	38.8	41.6	44.0	50.4	55.0	60.4	63.6	64.2	59.8	52.3	45.1	40.4	51.4

FORT KLAMATH, OREGON.

Year.	Jan.	Feb.	Mar.	Apr.	May.	June.	July.	Aug.	Sept.	Oct.	Nov.	Dec.	Annual.
1863												27.8	
1864	23.7	28.2	35.7	43.0	55.8	52.1	60.8	58.3	48.7	42.3	84.3	26.4	42.4
1865	21.0	19.2	30.5	34.7	43.4	52.5	61.1	52.3	47.2	39.0	35.0	20.7	36.6
1866	23.7	28.2	35.9										
1872	27.8	33.6							48.9	45.9	31.2		
1873	*26.6	27.5	36.8	36.8	47.2	53.6	64.2	63.3	87.9	44.8	30.9	26.3	44.2
1874	20.9	26.1	30.0	42.2	52.8	54.6	*61.5	57.5	55.1	47.6	35.7	28.8	43.2
1875	*26.6	28.4	33.0	48.4	49.6	56.4	63.8	62.6	55.2	48.7	34.0	35.0	45.0
1876	28.2	30.9	33.1	39.4	44.4	60.9	63.9	60.3	55.5	47.6	37.9	33.9	44.6
1877	28.6	35.4	41.8	42.1	47.2	56.4	61.8	61.6	51.7	42.4	35.5	24.6	44.4
1878	28.4	37.5	38.8	42.1	49.8	50.4	62.0	64.1	51.3	41.5	35.4	25.9	44.2
1879	10.8	*27.3	36.3	43.7	44.4	55.0	62.6	62.8	57.4	42.1	29.6	25.3	42.4
1880	26.2	23.2	26.0	35.1	44.5	50.6	62.7	57.4	52.1	*42.7	28.6	32.2	40.0
1881	30.8	32.9	*34.7	44.8	47.9	*56.8	54.7	52.1	46.9	34.7	26.0	26.0	40.0
1882	31.6	18.3	36.7	33.8	44.4	*55.8	60.6	57.8	51.2	38.5	31.6	36.3	36.2
1883	23.4	22.8	41.2	38.4	48.7	51.0	83.6	59.3	54.5	40.5	35.5	30.5	43.4
1884	24.2	22.5	33.4	41.0	52.5	54.0	58.9	64.2	48.2	41.6	37.3	27.9	42.2
1885	38.6	35.5	*34.8	45.0	52.1	54.9	53.1	62.7	52.2	47.5	36.0	34.8	45.7
1886	27.8	37.4	34.1	41.4	51.5	58.6	54.3	61.8	52.6	41.2	31.1	34.2	44.7
1887	30.7	22.9	38.6	40.9	51.7	57.0	64.7	61.4	54.9	46.2	34.9	27.4	44.3
Means	25.9	28.0	34.7	40.8	48.7	56.0	62.0	60.4	52.5	43.1	35.0	29.0	48.0

LA GRANDE, OREGON.

Year.	Jan.	Feb.	Mar.	Apr.	May.	June.	July.	Aug.	Sept.	Oct.	Nov.	Dec.	Annual.
1886							79.6	74.4	64.0	51.6	a43.8	b39.2	
1887	29.2	23.0	43.3	43.0	55.8	57.3	66.5	64.6	57.9	47.4	38.8	28.3	48.3
Means	29.2	29.0	43.3	43.0	55.8	57.3	73.0	69.5	62.0	49.5	41.2	33.8	48.4

LAKEVIEW, OREGON.

Year.	Jan.	Feb.	Mar.	Apr.	May.	June.	July.	Aug.	Sept.	Oct.	Nov.	Dec.	Annual.
1884	26.9	21.9	34.0	41.0	49.8	57.4	65.8	63.5	47.8	45.0	40.8	29.0	43.7
1885	31.1	38.3	46.3	48.2	51.6	*56.6	69.1	71.0	61.2	57.6	46.8	36.7	49.1
1886	32.0	44.0	35.6	43.6	53.9	58.7	65.4	64.3	58.9	44.4	34.3	37.4	47.4
1887	31.6	22.8	42.4	42.8	52.1	57.8	66.8	65.8	*56.0	50.4	38.4	*34.0	48.7
Means	30.8	31.8	39.6	43.9	51.8	58.0	66.6	66.2	54.0	49.4	38.4	34.0	47.2

LINKVILLE, OREGON.

Year.	Jan.	Feb.	Mar.	Apr.	May.	June.	July.	Aug.	Sept.	Oct.	Nov.	Dec.	Annual.
1884	28.6	26.2	37.1	42.0	53.7	55.5	61.2	65.6	48.8	43.8	42.3	28.4	44.5
1885	33.7	37.0	47.3	52.7	55.5	57.8	71.8	70.0	55.9	61.0	36.6	35.4	50.0
1886	30.7	43.0	38.0	45.8	55.4	60.8	64.4	65.4	57.1	46.9	37.8	41.3	49.0
1887	38.7	28.6	45.7	46.7	55.1	57.3	66.0	63.8	58.2	50.2	38.0	*35.4	48.5
Means	32.9	33.8	42.0	47.0	54.9	57.9	65.8	66.0	55.0	48.0	39.4	85.4	48.2

MOUNT ANGEL, OREGON.

Year.	Jan.	Feb.	Mar.	Apr.	May.	June.	July.	Aug.	Sept.	Oct.	Nov.	Dec.	Annual.
1886						65.3	69.8	68.2	52.6	50.0	41.5	48.0	
1887	43.6	34.5	48.0	49.3	56.0	61.5	67.7	66.0	60.5	52.0			
Means	43.6	34.5	48.0	49.3	56.0	63.4	68.8	67.1	61.6	51.0	41.5	48.0	52.7

NEWPORT, OREGON.

Year.	Jan.	Feb.	Mar.	Apr.	May.	June.	July.	Aug.	Sept.	Oct.	Nov.	Dec.	Annual.
1886	44.8	53.4	47.0	51.8	57+4	57.9	53.2	52.8	50.8	57.5	48.2	52.4	54.7
1887	47.2	37.6	50.2	52.7	58.6	59.7	50.9	61.2	51.3	51.7	45.9		
Means	46.0	45.5	48.6	52.2	57.7	61.9	51.5	62.0	55.6	54.6	47.0	52.4	53.7

*Interpolated.   a Observations for thirteen days.   b Observations for seventeen days.

Statement showing mean temperatures—Continued.

OREGON CITY, OREGON.

Year.	Jan.	Feb.	Mar.	Apr.	May.	June.	July.	Aug.	Sept.	Oct.	Nov.	Dec.	Annual
1849	32.4	36.0	40.8	57.1	59.7	66.0	72.3	73.5	62.7	57.1	48.7	37.9	53.5
1850	39.5	45.3	48.9	52.3	53.7	65.9	70.3	72.4	*60.2	55.9	48.7	38.5	54.9
1851	44.0	44.7	47.0	58.3	59.3	66.0	73.3	80.0	57.7	54.7	48.3	41.0	56.2
Means	38.8	42.0	45.2	55.9	60.9	66.3	72.0	71.6	60.2	55.8	47.2	39.1	54.8

PORT ORFORD, OREGON.

Year.	Jan.	Feb.	Mar.	Apr.	May.	June.	July.	Aug.	Sept.	Oct.	Nov.	Dec.	Annual
1852						66.5	61.3	62.7	59.2	54.7	60.6	44.2	
1853	48.7	46.5	47.9	51.6	57.1			59.1	59.5	54.8	45.1	53.3	48.2
1854							58.6	*60.2	59.6	56.8	56.9	47.0	52.2	53.6
1855	48.0	40.3	50.2	50.5	52.5	57.5	58.0						
1856	49.0	48.4	51.4	50.7	64.7	57.6		59.1	59.7	53.4	56.3	45.8	51.0
1875	43.3	46.4	54.8	49.9		59.2							
1876													
Means	47.2	47.6	51.1	50.7	54.8	58.8	59.1	60.4	57.5	55.8	49.9	49.2	53.5

PORTLAND, OREGON.

Year.	Jan.	Feb.	Mar.	Apr.	May.	June.	July.	Aug.	Sept.	Oct.	Nov.	Dec.	Annual
1868	38.1	30.9	42.5	61.5	55.6	66.8		67.7	64.4				41.5	
1869	43.7	42.2	42.7	52.9	58.7	68.4	72.9	71.8	63.8	53.2	48.4	37.1	54.2
1870	45.1	42.9	47.8	52.6	60.0	66.6	69.7	70.8	62.4	58.5	46.0	38.4	54.7
1871	38.0	42.8	45.2	47.8	56.0	62.3	66.3	64.0	59.1	52.5	42.3	42.2	51.7
1872	44.6	40.6	48.8	51.9	55.8	60.8	67.2	67.1	61.4	49.8	47.5	36.9	52.6
1873	42.9	43.7	46.1	53.9	59.7	60.2	68.3	64.7	61.4	56.1	45.3	42.6	53.7
1874	36.5	40.4	44.4	55.3	56.4	68.9	71.2	66.7	64.5	54.6	43.3	47.6	53.3
1875	30.0	45.2	44.9	50.4	55.5	65.1	66.6	64.1	62.9	57.6	45.8	40.2	53.1
1876	42.2	48.4	56.2	52.2	56.0	61.5	66.9	68.6	59.3	53.2	49.3	43.1	53.9
1877	40.6	46.1	51.0	51.8	54.5	64.8	64.8	66.3	59.5	51.4	47.2	40.2	53.3
1878	38.5	44.5	49.0	52.3	54.2	60.0	65.3	66.8	63.5	52.6	43.6	39.1	52.4
1879	42.0	37.6	41.2	49.4	53.0	68.5	54.6	62.9	59.1	52.9	43.4	40.0	50.4
1880	39.2	45.4	42.1	54.4	56.4	60.6	63.7	62.6	59.2	49.9	43.4	43.0	52.2
1881	39.3	27.7	43.7	46.5	56.3	62.6	65.3	64.8	59.4	50.8	43.6	45.9	51.5
1882	37.5	33.0	50.4	49.2	57.4	63.4	66.9	62.8	51.7	50.8	48.5	41.8	51.7
1883	38.7	28.0	45.4	54.0	58.8	62.7	63.5	68.0	53.7	51.2	46.7	31.0	51.1
1884	36.3	47.2	52.0	53.1	58.9	61.0	68.0	66.5	62.2	58.0	47.3	43.0	54.3
1885	36.1	44.7	44.8	49.9	57.7	62.9	67.4	64.8	57.4	51.4	41.6	45.5	52.8
1886	42.8	31.9	49.4	50.2	57.9	60.5	66.1	64.5	59.6	53.8	44.4	42.6	52.0
1887	30.0	44.0	46.2	55.0	62.3								
Means	39.2	41.6	46.9	51.9	57.2	62.7	67.0	65.9	60.9	53.0	45.2	41.1	52.7

ROSEBURGH, OREGON.

Year.	Jan.	Feb.	Mar.	Apr.	May.	June.	July.	Aug.	Sept.	Oct.	Nov.	Dec.	Annual
1877							67.3	67.1	60.9	52.5	48.0	42.7	
1878	44.0	47.8	51.4	61.1	56.1	68.5	64.3	66.3	58.7	46.5	46.1	38.1	53.1
1879	37.6	44.6	49.8	51.4	58.1	60.2	66.9	67.3	63.2	52.0	42.1	39.1	52.2
1880	41.3	37.1	40.1	48.7	52.6	59.3	67.0	64.4	60.0	51.3	38.7	45.5	50.8
1881	42.6	47.4	48.5	55.1	56.3	59.3	62.7	62.5	58.8	47.7	42.6	42.5	52.2
1882	38.6	30.1	43.9	48.6	55.5	53.9	67.5	64.9	58.7	56.8	47.4	44.6	51.5
1883	37.5	37.2	51.3	48.8	56.8	63.9	67.0	63.3	60.3	48.9	45.4	46.0	51.8
1884	30.1	38.4	45.7	51.4	58.0	61.0	63.4	*65.2	*60.8	51.2	47.4	37.4	51.6
1885	43.4	48.0	50.8	53.0	58.3	59.2	67.3	65.6	62.3	58.3	48.0	44.7	54.7
1886	41.2	45.4	45.1	49.5	60.7	61.5	67.4	66.2	61.4	56.7	40.9	47.0	52.8
1887	43.4	32.6	49.6	50.3	57.3	60.3	66.1	64.7	61.5	53.7	45.6	43.1	52.4
1888	35.1	44.5	47.2	56.0	60.1								
Means	40.3	42.1	47.6	51.3	56.6	61.1	66.0	65.2	60.8	51.4	44.4	42.2	52.4

SALEM, OREGON.

Year.	Jan.	Feb.	Mar.	Apr.	May.	June.	July.	Aug.	Sept.	Oct.	Nov.	Dec.	Annual
1856										70.5	56.2	50.3	
1857	41.3	49.2	46.5	49.5	58.4	64.5	67.1	68.3	65.2				
1858										49.5			
Means	41.3	49.2	46.5	49.5	58.4	64.5	67.1	68.3	65.2	60.0	56.2	50.3	56.8

* Interpolated.

CLIMATE OF OREGON AND WASHINGTON TERRITORY.

Statement showing mean temperatures—Continued.

FORT STEVENS, OREGON.

Year.	Jan.	Feb.	Mar.	Apr.	May.	June.	July.	Aug.	Sept.	Oct.	Nov.	Dec.	Annual.
1865											40.1	36.3	
1866	29.3	38.8	45.3	47.4	52.4	*58.9	*62.9	*61.4	58.3	53.9	49.8	44.4	51.1
1867	43.7	41.2	40.3	48.8	54.8	56.8	63.8	61.3	59.5	83.0	49.6	43.7	61.6
1868	31.9	41.3	44.7	56.6	53.5	58.6	62.0	61.4	56.8	*58.8	*47.3	*45.0	50.6
1869				51.8	56.5	50.5							
1871							66.8	61.8	58.2	54.2	46.1	38.6	
1872	41.6	45.5	40.5	48.8	54.3	58.7	61.4	60.0	56.5	54.6	42.3	42.3	51.3
1873	44.7	39.6	46.5	46.8	55.2	58.0	66.0	61.2	57.1	50.2	46.6	38.3	50.4
1874	46.9	40.7	43.0	56.9	55.4	56.8	59.5	66.5	56.6	54.2	44.7	43.5	50.7
1875	34.2	40.7	42.7	50.3	51.3	54.5	59.4	59.2	59.8	56.4	44.3	46.5	49.9
1876	38.6	44.7	43.5	48.3	52.2	59.4	60.2	56.0	60.6	55.3	47.2	40.6	50.7
1877	42.1	44.5	49.8	49.2	53.2	56.8	60.8	66.0	57.6	52.6	49.3	43.9	51.5
1878	44.2	45.5	45.8	49.6	54.6	58.9	59.8	59.1	57.3	50.5	47.6	41.4	51.3
1879	38.4	43.4	47.2	49.4	52.4	56.2	57.3	58.9	53.5	47.0	43.9	39.4	49.1
1880	36.8	38.8	41.4	47.3	56.5	54.7	68.0	59.1	56.8	61.7	42.3	40.4	48.4
1881	39.0	43.2	48.2	50.7	55.3	57.6	57.3	58.1	55.9	46.8	43.4	47.8	49.9
1882	39.8	37.2	42.0	46.1	56.5	52.8	53.3	54.8	*57.7	50.5	44.0	44.8	47.8
1883	37.8	35.8	46.7	47.3	52.7								
Means	39.7	41.5	45.6	49.1	53.3	57.3	59.8	59.6	57.7	52.4	46.0	42.0	50.3

THE DALLES, OREGON.

Year.	Jan.	Feb.	Mar.	Apr.	May.	June.	July.	Aug.	Sept.	Oct.	Nov.	Dec.	Annual.
1875	22.5	35.5	44.0	56.6	53.0	70.0	77.5	77.5	71.0	60.0	39.0	46.5	54.3
1876	27.0	46.5	44.0	50.1	59.5	75.5	78.0	70.5	67.5	55.0	44.5	37.5	54.7
1877	35.6	40.0	42.0	55.0	58.0	71.5	78.5	80.5	59.5	49.5	42.5	30.0	54.1
1878	36.0	43.0	54.0	53.0	61.5	74.6	73.0	71.6	63.6	48.0	46.5	40.0	55.3
1879	26.5	38.5	50.0	54.0	58.0	00.0	72.0	72.0	65.5	44.5	37.5	23.0	50.8
1880	46.5	45.0	41.0	55.5	66.5	68.6	73.5	70.5	60.5	54.0	39.0	24.0	53.0
1881	31.6	36.0	52.0	57.0	58.5	60.0	72.0	68.5	62.0	44.5	43.0	37.5	52.4
1882	28.0	29.8	48.0	57.0	62.0	71.5	72.5	68.5	61.0	49.0	34.0	35.5	51.4
1883	23.5	18.5	52.0	53.0	60.0	67.5	74.0	65.5	61.0	48.0	44.5	34.0	50.1
1884	21.6	18.0	43.0	56.0	62.5	71.0	70.5	74.5	60.0	56.5	42.5	16.0	49.9
1885	26.0	42.1	52.0	56.0	64.5	67.0	76.0	72.0	64.0	54.5	42.5	41.0	54.7
1886	22.8	42.5	46.6	50.0	61.0	70.0	71.0	73.5	61.0	51.0	38.5	20.0	52.1
1887	30.5	34.5	46.0	52.5	64.0	68.0	71.5	68.5	67.5	47.5	40.5	35.5	51.2
Means	29.9	35.4	47.2	54.0	60.6	69.7	73.7	71.8	62.6	50.5	40.9	34.6	52.5

CAMP THREE FORKS, OREGON.

Year.	Jan.	Feb.	Mar.	Apr.	May.	June.	July.	Aug.	Sept.	Oct.	Nov.	Dec.	Annual.
1868	15.5	29.4	36.5	44.0	47.9	56.9	87.7	72.0	62.7	53.8	44.6	43.8	47.1
1869	30.0	30.4	58.7	43.6	58.2	80.2	72.3	70.5	60.8	51.4	39.4	28.6	49.4
Means	22.8	29.9	37.1	43.8	53.0	83.0	70.0	71.2	61.8	52.6	41.7	31.1	48.2

UMATILLA, OREGON.

Year.	Jan.	Feb.	Mar.	Apr.	May.	June.	July.	Aug.	Sept.	Oct.	Nov.	Dec.	Annual.
1877	36.1	45.1	51.5	52.9	61.9	71.3	78.6	74.4	63.0	51.0	44.2	*36.0	
1878	37.6	38.5	49.7	54.2	57.6	86.3	73.4	75.1	61.8	51.7	43.6	22.8	54.9
1879	29.9	33.8	41.8	61.3	56.1	64.7	72.6	75.8	68.5	51.8	37.1	30.1	52.2
1880	38.5	34.5	48.2	55.2	54.2	64.1	69.0	67.1	62.7	52.1	55.6	20.8	52.6
1881	33.5	35.9	44.0	50.4	59.0	66.4	73.0	71.2	61.1	49.3	40.5	36.1	50.7
1882	28.5	15.6	46.4						64.1	50.8	37.8	40.0	52.4
Means	32.1	33.4	47.1	53.0	58.6	67.2	72.6	72.1	63.5	52.6	43.1	34.1	52.5

FORT UMPQUA, OREGON.

Year.	Jan.	Feb.	Mar.	Apr.	May.	June.	July.	Aug.	Sept.	Oct.	Nov.	Dec.	Annual.
1856								58.5	58.8	51.7	47.7	44.6	
1857	40.8	47.3	61.1	54.2	56.9	61.3	80.6	58.1	60.2	57.1	50.9	48.9	54.4
1858	46.1	47.9	48.9	51.5	55.9	59.0	59.6	60.6	59.3	54.3	50.7	44.3	50.3
1859	44.1	44.7	45.1	49.4	53.0	61.0	59.6	58.0	53.3	48.1	43.5	41.4	51.4
1860	46.7	47.5	47.9	50.3	54.1	56.0	66.3	60.7	56.8	54.1	51.2	46.1	63.0
1861	45.4	48.2	48.2	50.9	54.3	58.0	60.8	61.1	54.4	54.1	48.7	45.3	52.8
1862	36.0	41.0	47.5	47.8	52.0								
Means	44.2	46.1	48.1	50.7	54.5	59.5	59.9	60.7	58.0	54.0	49.0	45.5	52.5

* Interpolated.   a Observations for twenty-three days.

*Statement showing mean temperatures—*Continued.

CAMP WARNER, OREGON.

Year.	Jan.	Feb.	Mar.	Apr.	May.	June.	July.	Aug.	Sept.	Oct.	Nov.	Dec.	Annual.
1868	16.2	36.3	38.8	40.5	42.7	50.1	63.7	66.8	57.2	48.6	36.5	33.9	43.4
1869	26.9	27.2	37.1	43.3	54.9	57.1	68.4	63.7	56.1	48.5	37.6	28.4	46.6
1870	32.4	38.7	31.6	45.4	51.7	60.2	70.8	69.4	50.4	48.9	40.6	28.2	47.0
1871	34.0	33.0	37.6	43.7	51.4	63.7	68.5	68.9	58.4	47.6	35.1	23.8	48.1
1872	26.6	32.3	36.8	36.5	52.1	61.2	67.5	64.1	54.0	48.6	32.3	31.3	45.7
1873	34.3	30.3	36.1	38.5	45.9	56.7	68.4	64.0	56.1	43.0	42.2	24.6	45.0
1874	29.4	34.9	27.2	37.4	48.9	53.6	69.1	a 58.9	......	......	......	......	......
Means	28.9	30.9	34.6	40.5	48.6	56.2	68.1	65.2	57.0	47.5	37.4	30.1	45.7

CAMP WATSON, OREGON.

Year.	Jan.	Feb.	Mar.	Apr.	May.	June.	July.	Aug.	Sept.	Oct.	Nov.	Dec.	Annual.
1867	*29.0	*26.9	*36.1	43.2	52.7	59.6	61.7	67.2	58.0	43.2	39.5	32.6	46.1
1868	12.1	26.4	36.2	42.8	46.5	65.0	64.2	65.0	54.3	44.8	36.8	23.6	43.0
1869	29.0	28.9	37.0	44.0	......	......	......	......	......	......	......	......	......
Means	23.4	26.1	36.1	43.6	49.6	57.4	63.0	66.1	56.6	44.0	37.8	33.2	44.9

FORT YAMHILL, OREGON.

Year.	Jan.	Feb.	Mar.	Apr.	May.	June.	July.	Aug.	Sept.	Oct.	Nov.	Dec.	Annual.
1856	......	......	......	......	......	......	......	......	......	49.2	43.7	38.9	......
1857	34.8	41.6	47.4	53.5	57.3	57.6	62.3	60.0	57.2	52.4	43.6	42.4	51.4
1858	68.4	40.6	43.9	46.0	52.9	56.6	59.3	51.9	58.4	47.8	43.9	35.8	49.0
1859	37.4	38.1	40.8	45.9	51.9	62.3	58.1	60.7	57.5	52.5	36.2	34.7	48.2
1860	30.7	42.2	44.5	46.4	50.3	56.9	61.0	66.2	59.5	53.6	45.3	39.3	50.3
1861	40.4	42.7	44.1	47.9	50.1	46.0	63.7	71.8	56.4	50.4	*43.5	34.6	50.0
1862	23.9	32.8	40.0	43.6	51.5	57.6	60.4	50.2	57.0	51.3	42.7	39.6	45.9
1863	40.0	34.7	45.6	47.3	*58.9	56.6	64.9	60.1	50.0	50.2	43.2	42.1	49.9
1864	38.1	44.2	45.1	46.6	57.8	56.7	51.6	60.3	58.6	52.7	43.7	38.8	50.4
1865	36.9	37.2	40.9	45.6	55.6	58.2	60.8	61.1	58.3	52.5	47.6	53.4	48.7
1866	37.6	37.8	44.8	46.1	......	......	......	......	......	......	......	......	......
Means	37.1	39.6	43.6	47.8	53.5	57.0	60.9	61.2	58.1	51.2	43.5	38.2	49.3

BOISÉ CITY, IDAHO.

Year.	Jan.	Feb.	Mar.	Apr.	May.	June.	July.	Aug.	Sept.	Oct.	Nov.	Dec.	Annual.
1877	......	......	......	......	......	......	73.0	72.4	60.8	49.4	41.6	31.5	......
1878	34.5	49.6	49.1	50.1	57.1	66.7	73.9	75.1	59.5	47.8	42.5	30.4	52.4
1879	36.5	39.9	47.3	56.8	54.7	63.8	73.0	74.1	66.1	48.7	37.1	31.1	51.4
1880	27.9	32.3	36.4	48.4	53.0	64.0	71.6	68.9	59.3	47.8	31.5	35.0	48.9
1881	36.5	36.7	44.3	51.0	66.4	64.4	71.3	67.3	56.6	45.8	36.2	33.0	50.0
1882	34.9	30.0	38.8	47.6	57.5	66.1	76.1	72.6	60.4	48.6	36.1	22.0	48.6
1883	21.6	21.3	46.2	44.2	56.0	66.5	b 73.2	73.2	62.0	44.5	36.3	......	......
1884	28.0	30.7	43.6	52.0	61.1	67.1	72.4	73.6	54.6	51.3	30.3	26.1	50.0
1885	34.0	38.4	46.0	52.7	58.9	64.3	72.9	71.5	61.6	52.6	45.8	35.3	52.1
1886	28.2	39.9	40.0	47.5	59.1	66.9	75.0	73.7	59.1	48.9	33.4	37.7	50.8
1887	36.2	30.1	47.6	48.3	60.3	62.6	73.8	70.5	63.2	50.5	38.3	32.6	51.4
1888	17.7	40.3	42.7	56.5	56.9	......	......	......	......	......	......	......	......
Means	28.1	34.7	43.6	50.5	57.8	65.6	73.0	72.1	60.3	48.5	38.4	32.7	50.5

* Interpolated.　　a Observations for twenty-two days.　　b Observations for sixteen days.

APPENDIX No. 5.

Temperature data for Washington Territory.

Name of station.	County.	Latitude.	Longitude.	Elevation.	Length.	From—	To (inclusive)—	Remarks as to observers and character of records.
		° ′	° ′	*Feet.*	*Yrs. Mos.*			
Bainbridge Island	Kitsap...........	47 32	122 40	50	10 6	Jan., 1878	Dec., 1887	R. M. Hoskinson.
Bellingham, Fort	Whatcom........	48 45	122 30	86	2 7	Jan., 1857	July, 1859	United States post hospital.
Cape Disappointment (or Fort Canby).	Pacific........	46 17	124 02	30	20 6	July, 1864	May, 1888	July, 1864, to Aug., 1883, United States post hospital. Sept., 1883, to May, 1888. Signal Service.
Cascades, Fort	Skamania	45 39	121 50	......	3 1	May, 1858	May, 1861	United States post hospital.
Cathlamet (near)	Wahkiakum	46 15	123 12	40	6 5	Jan., 1870	Aug., 1878	C. McCall.
Colville, Fort..........	Stevens..........	48 42	118 02	1,963	18 3	Nov., 1859	Feb., 1880	Nov. and Dec., 1859, report Northwest Boundary. Jan., 1860, to Feb., 1880, United States post hospital.
Dayton	Columbia........	46 19	117 58	1,080	6 1	Dec., 1879	Dec., 1885	Signal Service.
George, Fort	Cowlitz........	46 18	123 00	......	2 0	June, 1821	Mar., 1824	Scouler. Edinburgh Journal of Science, vol. 6, observations at 6 a. m., noon, and 6 p/m.
Kennewick	Yakima	46 15	119 15	353	3 2	Nov., 1884	Dec., 1887	A. W. Gray.
Kooskooskee	Lewis..........	46 30	122 37	......	2 0	....	....	H. W. Dove. Klimatologische Beiträge,[pages 42, 43, 1857; observations at sunrise, 2 p. m., sunset, and 9 p. m.
Neah Bay	Clallam..........	48 22	124 37	40	12 4	June, 1862	May, 1888	J. G. Swan. June, 1862, to July 1881. Signal Service, Jan., 18-4. to May, 1888.
New Tacoma	Pierce	47 10	122 26	297	4 0	June, 1881	Dec., 1887	E. N. Fuller.
Olympia.	Thurston	47 3	122 53	36	10 11	July, 1877	May, 1888	Signal Service.
Pleasant Grove.......	Kittitass	47 00	120 30	1,500	2 4	Jan., 1884	Apr., 1886	George W. Parrish.
Port Angeles (Ediz Hook Light Station).	Clallam........	48 08	123 24	12	4 5	Jan., 1881	May, 1888	Jan. to Dec., 1881. Thomas Stratton. Jan., 1885, to May, 1888, Signal Service.
San Juan Island	San Juan	48 28	123 01	150	13 8	Jan., 1860	June, 1874	United States post hospital.
Semiahmoo, Camp	Whatcom........	49 01	122 46	11	3 0	July, 1857	June, 1860	Report of Northwest Boundary Commission. Observations twice hourly, from 6 a. m. to 10 p. m. during 1857–1858. In 1859 hourly in Jan., Feb., and Mar., and in Apr. hourly, 6 a. m. to 10 p. m.
Simcoe, Fort..........	Yakima........	46 14	120 40	......	2 4	Jan., 1857	Apr., 1860	United States post hospital.
Steilacoom, Fort......	Pierce..........	47 10	122 25	300	15 8	Nov., 1849	Nov., 1868	United States post hospital; Nov., 1849, to Dec., 1854, observations at sunrise, 9 a. m., 3 p. m., and 9 p. m.
Spokane Falls	Spokane........	47 40	117 25	1,900	7 5	Jan., 1841	May, 1878	Signal Service.
Spokane, Fort	......do	47 30	118 30	1,680	4 0	Jan., 1882	Dec., 1887	Do.
Yatcooh Island Light House.	Clallam........	48 23	124 44	90	7 9	Jan., 1860	May, 1888	Jan., 1860, to Jan., 1872, A. Sampson. Oct., 1845, to May, 1888, Signal Service.
Townsend, Fort	Jefferson	48 05	122 48	125	15 7	Jan., 1859	Dec., 1887	United States post hospital.
Union Ridge..........	Clarke.........	45 49	122 42	100	1 0	July, 1871	June, 1872	T. H. Whitcomb.
Vancouver, Fort........	.....do	45 40	122 30	56	18 0	Dec., 1849	July, 1868	United States post hospital ; Dec., 1849, to Dec., 1854, sunrise, 9 a. m., 2 p. m., 9 p. m.
Walla Walla..........	Walla Walla.....	46 05	118 54	930	4 7	Nov., 1869	May, 1888	Nov., 1869, to Nov., 1879, A. H. Simmons. Dec., 1885, to May, 1888, Signal Service.
Walla Walla, Fort.....	.....do	46 03	118 20	......	14 6	Jan., 1857	Dec., 1887	United States post hospital.
Helena, Mont..........	Lewis and Clarke	46 34	112 4	4,069	8 2	Apr., 1880	May, 1888	Signal Service.

NOTE.—Where not otherwise mentioned observations were taken at 7 a. m., 2 p. m., and 9 p. m.

Statement showing mean temperatures—Continued.

BAINBRIDGE ISLAND, WASH.

Year.	Jan.	Feb.	Mar.	Apr.	May.	June.	July.	Aug	Sept.	Oct.	Nov.	Dec.	Annual.
1878	*39.1	45.1	50.8	52.5	57.3	62.0	68.5	62.5	57.5	50.0	48.1	41.5	52.3
1879	36.1	48.1	47.8	50.0	53.0	56.0	61.1	63.0	58.5	51.5	42.3	40.0	50.8
1880	38.0	42.0	42.0	48.5	52.1	61.3	63.6	62.0	54.0	72.2	41.1	40.1	50.1
1881	30.5	45.2	50.0	52.0	58.0	60.0	62.5	61.1	56.3	50.0	46.1	44.0	51.0
1882	39.0	38.7	44.2	40.0	56.7	62.7	63.0	56.0	57.5	52.0	45.5	46.0	51.3
1883	38.7	38.0	49.3	53.1	58.3	61.0	62.5	62.5	56.0	46.3	44.3	41.3	51.0
1884	39.0	34.6	43.0	51.3	52.7	60.2	62.5	63.0	54.0	42.0	47.2	33.0	49.2
1885	39.0	44.6	47.5	50.0	57.7	63.5	65.7	62.5	60.0	52.0	47.3	43.6	52.9
1886	37.0	43.5	44.0	50.0	50.7	62.3	63.0	56.0	48.5	53.2	44.7	48.2	51.8
1887	42.2	32.7	46.8	49.5	56.2	59.5	62.0	61.2	57.2	50.0	43.0	42.0	50.2
Means	38.1	41.1	46.5	50.7	55.6	61.2	63.1	62.6	56.4	50.6	44.9	41.8	51.1

FORT BELLINGHAM, WASH.

Year.	Jan.	Feb.	Mar.	Apr.	May.	June.	July.	Aug	Sept.	Oct.	Nov.	Dec.	Annual.
1857	*39.3	*42.6	47.4	54.8	59.9	64.3	81.4	62.2	57.4	52.3	43.8	42.6	52.1
1858	41.0	37.3	45.1	48.1	54.4	59.6	60.0	62.2	58.6	48.0	45.2	37.0	49.8
1859	39.0	38.9	41.5	47.9	53.4	50.4	61.1						
Means	37.8	39.6	44.7	50.3	55.9	61.1	62.1	62.2	58.0	50.2	44.5	39.8	50.5

CAPE DISAPPOINTMENT, OR FORT CANBY, WASH.

Year.	Jan.	Feb.	Mar.	Apr.	May.	June.	July.	Aug	Sept.	Oct.	Nov.	Dec.	Annual.
1864								80.7	64.1	50.8	56.8	50.0	48.8	
1865	42.4	41.0	42.0	46.6	57.6	61.4	63.2	*60.0	*58.0	54.0	49.4	*47.2	52.9
1866							50.5	62.5	60.7	56.8	53.7	50.8	48.9	
1867	42.6	41.2	40.3	45.8	56.3	58.9	63.6	58.0	54.5	53.6	50.4	45.3	51.7
1868	34.4	43.3	46.7	58.1	68.2	58.1	61.0	60.0	58.8	54.2	51.0	49.0	52.0
1869	45.4	44.0	51.9	50.9									
1871					62.7	58.0	60.0	61.0	58.1	54.0	47.9	42.0	
1872	44.4	45.5	47.8	49.0	55.1	50.2	59.9	56.3	54.5	50.2	42.1		
1873	41.9	36.2	49.0	46.9	49.0	53.0							54.0
1874	37.6	36.4	38.6	47.0	53.6	54.2							
1875	29.6	41.8	41.1	46.2	54.0	58.2	62.0	63.0	50.3	56.4	45.8	47.0	50.3
1876	40.5	44.0	43.9	49.3	52.9	58.4	60.1	58.6	60.2	56.0	48.1	43.5	51.5
1877	45.0	46.1	43.8	51.3	53.7	57.9	62.1	60.6	57.1	57.1	49.6	45.6	52.7
1878	40.1	40.7	50.0	50.4	55.3	58.5	60.1	60.2	56.4	50.4	48.8	40.9	52.1
1879	39.3	43.3	46.6	49.3	52.5	58.4	57.0	58.5	57.2	51.1	43.9	44.0	49.9
1880	41.0	39.3	42.1	47.5	51.0	54.2	58.5	60.6	56.4	57.8	43.2	43.0	48.7
1881	42.0	45.8	48.0	52.1	54.2	67.9	58.1	60.7	57.6	51.3	45.9	45.1	51.6
1882	41.1	39.6	43.4	47.2	54.8	50.6	50.9	61.6	50.1	51.4	45.3	46.0	50.7
1883	46.3	38.6	48.8	48.9	54.4	57.5	61.1	63.4	60.6	51.1	47.3	41.3	51.1
1884	42.6	38.2	44.0	50.5	53.4	55.2	58.6	60.7	55.3	52.5	50.9	36.5	49.9
1885	41.7	45.7	49.5	48.9	52.0	55.8	60.4	57.8	58.5	55.1	49.5	48.7	51.8
1886	40.1	46.6	44.1	48.1	52.1	56.1	50.0	60.5	58.3	52.4	45.8	47.5	50.8
1887	43.2	34.4	45.4	46.3	52.0	54.1	56.0	56.8	55.4	53.2	46.5	43.8	48.8
1888	36.5	43.3	43.9	48.1	58.1								
Means	40.8	42.0	45.3	49.1	53.4	57.4	60.3	60.2	57.9	53.6	48.6	44.2	51.0

FORT CASCADES, WASH.

Year.	Jan.	Feb.	Mar.	Apr.	May.	June.	July.	Aug	Sept.	Oct.	Nov.	Dec.	Annual.
1858					57.4	65.0	85.5	67.4	62.2	48.6	45.2	34.6	
1859	31.9	39.5	39.6	49.8	55.3	64.5	86.0	61.3	50.8	55.5	30.8	30.2	49.7
1860	37.0	43.3	47.8	50.0	53.9	61.0	65.1	59.1	62.2	54.6	43.9	39.2	52.5
1861	37.9	44.8	47.7	51.4	54.6								
Means	36.3	41.5	45.1	50.4	55.3	63.5	65.5	86.0	61.5	53.2	43.5	34.7	51.5

NEAR CATHLAMET, WASH.

Year.	Jan.	Feb.	Mar.	Apr.	May.	June.	July.	Aug	Sept.	Oct.	Nov.	Dec.	Annual.
1870	*38.2	*40.4	40.0	48.4	58.6	50.2	85.0	64.4				35.4	
1871	42.3	39.8	43.9	48.3	51.0	58.2	60.4	61.0	57.0	49.2	48.7	38.2	49.4
1872	30.2	43.3	48.9	45.0	52.8	57.2	61.4	59.4	50.0	51.0	40.6	45.0	49.6
1873	42.7	37.5	44.8	47.8	52.2	55.4	61.0	60.7	56.8	47.2	*43.6	*40.4	49.1
1874	36.8	40.7	42.4	50.0	50.2	57.3	61.6	61.7	58.6	*51.0	46.4	42.2	50.7
1875	32.0	38.3	41.5	53.5	52.2	57.3	62.2	58.0	56.3	55.9	44.4	45.7	50.4
1876	37.2	42.9	42.7	49.1	52.8	60.6	61.0	00.4					
Means	38.2	40.4	43.2	49.1	52.9	57.9	61.8	61.4	58.0	51.0	43.8	40.4	49.6

* Interpolated.

Statement showing mean temperatures—Continued.

COLVILLE DEPOT AND FORT COLVILLE, WASH.

Year.	Jan.	Feb.	Mar.	Apr.	May.	June.	July.	Aug.	Sept.	Oct.	Nov.	Dec.	Annual.
1859												22.5	16.8
1860	23.8	31.3	a38.2	a45.1	a43.5	a61.9	a68.6	70.1	56.4	47.0	36.6	28.7	41.6
1861	26.2	30.8	36.7	45.5	51.7	60.4	67.9	64.3	51.6	41.4	34.0	27.0	41.3
1862	2.5	15.0	31.4	43.2	57.7	65.6	65.9	66.5	56.1	42.7	29.6	27.1	42.0
1863	23.3	26.4	34.3	46.2	55.8	67.6	72.4	50.6	53.6	38.3	26.6	34.8	44.6
1864	21.2	29.9	35.5	48.5	64.4	65.2	77.6	65.9					
1866										41.2	37.8	29.4	
1867	34.7	26.3	19.6	42.1	51.4	63.4	64.4	71.6	58.7	43.3	34.8	36.4	44.4
1868	7.0	18.7	20.5	56.9	54.9	65.2	70.6	60.4	50.8	42.6	32.6	26.5	44.9
1869	26.9	26.8	34.1	47.8	61.8	70.6	76.9	60.6	55.1	43.1	35.3	30.3	45.8
1870	24.8	30.4	32.3	46.3	55.9	64.0	71.2	67.7	58.7	45.5	33.4	22.3	48.4
1871	27.7	25.8	36.2	46.1	60.7	69.0	73.2	68.0	60.7	47.8	33.9	22.7	47.7
1872	22.8	30.9	36.6	43.8	56.3	64.2	71.4	64.7	55.2	43.5	25.8	20.8	45.0
1873	25.2	25.4	37.4	45.6	53.0	58.1	68.3	67.7	57.8	42.4	33.5	20.3	45.0
1874	25.2	28.3	32.5	45.8	57.5	58.2	67.4	64.7	55.1	46.6	27.3	24.9	44.9
1875	5.7	21.8	31.4	47.7	51.8	56.9	72.2	69.2	58.2	50.0	26.2	33.1	44.0
1876	15.7	35.5	31.2	44.1	54.8	54.3	67.9	53.2	56.4	50.3	33.0	24.4	45.2
1877	22.6	32.6	38.2	47.4	54.6	59.1	67.7	67.8	54.6	43.5	38.2	27.6	45.9
1878	27.4	*27.5	36.6	46.4	55.8	65.7	67.7	70.5	54.9	41.8	35.4	24.6	47.5
1879	21.1	27.8	37.2	46.1	51.7	59.4	65.0	58.2	64.0	41.5	30.8	18.4	44.3
1880	34.3	28.5											
Means	20.6	27.5	35.3	46.7	55.5	63.5	69.3	66.7	56.6	44.2	32.3	23.8	45.3

DAYTON, WASH.

Year	Jan	Feb	Mar	Apr	May	June	July	Aug	Sept	Oct	Nov	Dec	Annual
1878												30.6	
1879	38.3	32.8	38.4	48.0	52.8	61.5	67.4	63.9	50.0	51.8	32.6	28.8	47.9
1881	27.6	37.6	46.9	53.4	56.3	60.8	67.0	61.8	57.5	46.7	36.1	37.1	48.3
1882	31.6	32.6	41.0	46.2	54.4	63.6	67.7	66.4	60.0	45.9	35.4	38.3	48.6
1883	36.5	17.6	43.6	46.1	56.4	65.0	60.9	68.2	59.9	45.6	43.0	32.8	48.1
1884	30.5	24.8	39.9	50.7	59.7	61.0	64.8	70.4	54.4	50.8	40.0	15.8	47.7
1885	26.0	42.1	46.6	50.7	57.3	61.7	69.7	78.1	66.3	52.0	44.3	*30.5	51.1
Means	30.1	31.3	43.4	49.2	56.2	62.8	67.6	67.3	58.8	48.8	38.6	30.5	48.7

FORT GEORGE, WASH.

	Jan	Feb	Mar	Apr	May	June	July	Aug	Sept	Oct	Nov	Dec	Annual
Means	36.1	42.4	44.8	48.7	58.0	59.6	61.4	62.7	59.5	56.1	47.6	39.7	51.6

KENNEWICK, WASH.

Year	Jan	Feb	Mar	Apr	May	June	July	Aug	Sept	Oct	Nov	Dec	Annual
1884										40.0	16.0		
1885	22.5	38.0	56.6	56.0	66.0	74.6	78.8	86.6	61.5	53.5	37.0	58.5	
1886	24.6	43.5	48.6	54.6	62.5	73.0	70.5	78.6	62.5	54.5	43.8	55.8	
1887	*28.2	21.5	50.6	55.6	68.0	66.0	75.0	72.8	69.5	46.5	40.5	*32.7	51.4
Means	23.2	34.3	51.3	54.5	64.5	71.6	77.5	76.3	61.5	51.5	48.4	32.7	53.5

KOOSKOOSKEE, WASH.

	Jan	Feb	Mar	Apr	May	June	July	Aug	Sept	Oct	Nov	Dec	Annual
Means	31.8	27.6	44.8	52.8	57.8	69.4	70.5	72.7	68.5	49.0	42.4	41.5	58.2

NEAH BAY, WASH.

Year	Jan	Feb	Mar	Apr	May	June	July	Aug	Sept	Oct	Nov	Dec	Annual
1862						56.7	60.7	59.9	54.7	56.3	48.4	46.7	
1863					51.2	55.7	58.4	56.2	56.8	46.3	42.8	46.9	
1864	36.5	42.5	43.4	45.6	51.5	54.4	55.2	58.9	48.3	*33.3	42.4	36.8	47.3
1865	36.0	36.7	36.2	42.7	49.8	53.2	54.8	*57.3	53.6	49.1	45.8	35.1	46.0
1866	37.2	27.3	42.4	44.7	49.2	53.5	55.6	*57.7	52.8	44.8	*43.5	*40.1	47.0
1867	40.6	*38.8	37.3										
1874	*37.4	39.8	41.6	48.4	54.0	56.1	59.1	60.1	53.5	47.9	42.1	44.6	48.6
1875	32.7												
1876										46.6	40.4	37.7	
1879	36.2	37.7	42.2	45.0	50.7	54.2	56.0	57.2	56.5	48.1	43.7	37.0	48.6
1880	36.0	36.0	35.1	44.2	48.9	50.4	57.9	57.3	53.5	48.2	40.7	30.8	45.3
1881	30.0	43.0	44.6	48.3	49.8	54.0	55.6	58.9	54.6	56.0	43.5	34.4	49.7
1884	44.2	38.6	46.6	51.8	54.6	55.8	58.8	59.3	57.0	51.3	46.4	44.7	50.8
1885	36.7	44.8	46.4	48.3	53.4	56.7	58.4	59.3	58.8	56.0	44.2	47.7	49.6
1886	37.7	44.0	42.6	47.0	51.6	56.4	60.5	56.6	56.6	48.2			
1887	44.0	31.0											
1888	35.6	43.4	42.6	48.2	52.6								
Means	38.4	39.7	41.8	46.5	51.5	54.6	57.3	58.1	53.6	49.8	44.3	40.6	48.0

* Interpolated.   NOTE.—Means, 1884 to 1888, inclusive, from maximum and minimum readings.
a Observations at Harney's Depot, latitude 48° 34', longitude 117° 53'.

Statement showing mean temperatures—Continued.

NEW TACOMA, WASH.

Year.	Jan.	Feb.	Mar.	Apr.	May.	June.	July.	Aug.	Sept.	Oct.	Nov.	Dec.	Annual.
1861	a40.0		43.0			62.8	64.2	64.2	37.8	51.0			
1884						a64.0		65.0	54.2		45.8	20.0	
1885	27.8	45.0	47.0	54.0	57.6	60.0	66.4	64.5	58.8	51.4	45.6	41.4	52.5
1886	35.2	43.5	43.0	47.4	57.3	60.9	66.8	65.6	58.5	50.9	40.5	44.3	51.3
1887	39.8	30.1	45.2	47.1	58.0	58.9	66.4	60.5	57.9	50.2	42.3	40.6	49.2
Means	38.2	39.5	44.6	48.5	56.3	61.3	65.2	64.0	57.6	50.9	42.5	38.9	50.8

OLYMPIA, WASH.

Year.	Jan.	Feb.	Mar.	Apr.	May.	June.	July.	Aug.	Sept.	Oct.	Nov.	Dec.	Annual.
1877							68.7	62.0	55.4	49.6	45.9	42.6	
1878	41.3	44.0	47.7	42.0	55.0	60.0	60.8	64.0	54.5	47.8	45.6	46.1	50.8
1879	35.7	40.8	44.8	47.5	52.3	57.4	61.1	62.3	57.8	46.8	41.9	38.0	49.0
1880	36.9	36.6	39.5	48.7	50.3	57.0	61.5	58.7	54.8	48.4	39.8	40.6	47.7
1881	39.0	43.7	46.8	46.9	52.3	57.0	56.5	58.8	55.1	47.4	43.6	42.1	49.7
1882	38.1	36.7	41.0	45.6	52.3	60.2	61.9	60.9	56.4	48.8	40.9	42.5	48.9
1883	35.9	37.5	45.9	46.8	53.3	58.4	61.5	61.3	55.6	44.7	45.7	39.8	49.0
1884	30.1	34.0	42.4	51.0	56.1	58.5	61.2	65.7	54.9	50.1	47.0	32.7	49.4
1885	40.0	42.1	47.1	48.0	55.5	61.1	64.0	60.9	57.9	51.0	45.9	43.0	51.8
1886	36.8	43.3	42.4	47.8	54.7	59.9	63.4	63.4	54.8	48.5	42.1	44.6	50.3
1887	40.7	31.6	43.3	47.2	55.2	57.3	61.7	61.1	58.0	49.2	43.4	41.3	49.2
1888	32.5	42.2	43.7	60.4	57.4								
Means	37.8	39.2	44.3	48.3	54.1	58.8	61.9	62.0	56.0	49.0	43.8	40.7	49.7

PLEASANT GROVE, WASH.

Year.	Jan.	Feb.	Mar.	Apr.	May.	June.	July.	Aug.	Sept.	Oct.	Nov.	Dec.	Annual.
1884	*21.0	16.5	34.5	51.0	58.0	62.0	60.0	68.0	50.5	49.0	38.0	11.5	43.5
1885	22.0	35.0	47.0	50.5	57.0	62.5	66.5	b65.5	58.5	68.0	37.5	32.5	46.5
1886	20.0	34.5	39.5	53.5									
Means	21.6	28.7	40.3	51.7	57.5	62.2	63.2	66.6	54.5	48.5	37.8	22.0	45.9

PORT ANGELES, WASH.

Year.	Jan.	Feb.	Mar.	Apr.	May.	June.	July.	Aug.	Sept.	Oct.	Nov.	Dec.	Annual.
1883	*34.5	*38.1	*41.4	54.0	54.2	55.6	59.0	57.6	53.1	48.3	48.3	42.3	49.0
1885	*34.5	42.7	44.7	45.2	50.4	54.2	58.1	55.4	52.8	47.2	42.9	40.2	47.4
1886	33.2	40.3	39.7	44.2	48.0	53.8	56.9	55.8	52.1	45.0	39.5	43.8	45.9
1887	36.5	28.9	40.7	43.4	48.6	52.2	54.3	55.1	51.1	46.0	41.5	39.2	45.0
1888	31.7	40.5	40.7	46.1	50.7								
Means	34.5	38.1	41.4	47.0	51.2	54.0	57.1	56.0	52.3	46.6	42.3	40.8	46.8

SAN JUAN ISLAND, WASH.

Year.	Jan.	Feb.	Mar.	Apr.	May.	June.	July.	Aug.	Sept.	Oct.	Nov.	Dec.	Annual.
1860	*36.6	42.5	46.3	48.8	54.3	60.1	60.4	63.1	56.4	53.8	47.7	43.6	51.2
1861	39.2	42.0	44.2	47.8	52.8	57.6	60.0	59.0	57.9	49.7	42.8	29.3	49.4
1862	28.3	36.2	42.0	48.8	54.6	58.0	60.3	60.1	58.7	50.5	45.3	43.6	48.4
1863	42.0	36.2	44.2	50.6	54.5	58.9	64.3	59.3	57.5	49.9	44.4	42.6	50.6
1864	40.0	43.5	45.0	50.3	55.9	57.3	59.2	59.8	55.7	50.3	45.1	37.7	56.0
1865	38.8	36.8	37.6	47.1	54.9								34.7
1866	37.9	36.6	43.8	47.3					58.1	50.8	47.3	43.5	
1867	40.3	39.5	27.9	49.4	56.8	58.7	60.1	61.3	58.4	48.9	45.4	43.5	48.8
1868	31.1	40.4	44.9	50.0	54.9	60.9	62.5	62.1	54.5	50.2	46.0	42.7	50.0
1869	42.5	45.1	48.3	52.1	57.8	68.8	63.7	99.0	57.2	52.1	46.9	43.0	52.4
1870	46.0	41.4	46.0	45.6	56.0	61.2	66.1	64.6	56.6	51.2	48.4	39.4	51.0
1871	39.8	38.3	43.8	49.7	52.3	60.4	62.4	63.1	57.6	51.3	43.5	34.8	48.6
1872	40.9	42.6	47.1	47.9	53.7	60.7	64.0	59.8	57.1	54.4		38.8	50.9
1873	41.2	38.1	44.1	48.3	58.3	56.4	59.7	60.6			44.9		46.7
1874	*36.5	38.6	43.5	54.1	60.5	63.0							
Means	38.5	40.2	43.4	49.4	55.1	59.9	62.0	61.1	57.1	50.8	45.3	40.3	50.2

CAMP SEMIAHMOO, WASH.

Year.	Jan.	Feb.	Mar.	Apr.	May.	June.	July.	Aug.	Sept.	Oct.	Nov.	Dec.	Annual.
1857							62.2	60.6	54.3	48.9	40.1	39.2	
1858	37.5	33.0	42.6	46.6	54.0	58.3	60.5	58.5	56.6	47.3	43.8	34.9	47.8
1859	36.5	38.0	41.3	47.5	55.0	62.4	64.8	63.9	58.0	48.6	37.1	38.6	44.9
1860	37.2	41.6	44.9	48.4	54.3	63.3							
Means	36.7	37.6	42.9	47.5	54.3	61.3	62.5	61.0	56.3	48.6	40.3	35.9	46.3

* Interpolated.   a Observations from maximum and minimum thermometers.   b Observations for twenty-one days.

*Statement showing mean temperatures—*Continued.

FORT SIMCOE, WASH.

Year.	Jan.	Feb.	Mar.	Apr.	May	June.	July.	Aug.	Sept.	Oct.	Nov.	Dec.	Annual.
1857	*30.3	*31.8	*40.7	54.9	61.8	67.6	70.9	70.7	60.8	51.7	36.3	36.4	51.1
1858	31.9	31.6	42.4	52.2	60.2	64.7	73.7	74.7	66.1	48.8	41.7	28.1	51.0
1859	28.7	32.3	38.0	51.9									
Means	30.3	31.8	40.7	52.0	61.0	67.8	72.0	72.7	64.4	50.2	39.0	32.8	51.3

FORT STEILACOOM, WASH.

Year	Jan.	Feb.	Mar.	Apr.	May	June.	July.	Aug.	Sept.	Oct.	Nov.	Dec.	Annual.
1849											46.8	36.3	
1850	35.9	39.1	40.5	47.3	55.0	61.1	64.2	63.4	56.5	51.9	41.2	37.2	49.5
1851	40.6	40.3	43.2	51.3	54.4	61.9	62.9	66.6	57.0	52.9	46.3	41.2	51.8
1852	43.5	42.6	40.3	46.5	57.1	68.0	58.5	63.9	57.1	51.7	43.6	33.3	50.5
1853	38.7	39.8	41.9	46.7	57.6	60.5	66.7	62.1	68.8	53.6	45.1	44.6	51.6
1854	30.0	30.6	48.9	50.8	55.6	58.0	65.7	62.6	56.6	51.7	46.7	48.1	50.6
1855	42.0	43.2	47.8	48.4	54.6	56.1	*64.6	66.3	*56.9	56.6	44.9	34.5	51.7
1856	42.2	48.2	47.7	51.1	56.2	58.6	62.1	64.7	59.2	51.4	43.8	37.8	51.7
1857	36.6	40.7	41.7	51.4	56.3	57.7	61.4	61.2	56.1	50.7	42.6	41.3	49.9
1858	38.0	36.8	44.2	48.6	54.7	61.4	60.7	62.2	58.6	46.9	44.3	37.7	49.5
1859	36.3	36.9	37.8	45.2	50.7	60.0	61.9	60.8	57.6	51.6	37.4	35.6	48.3
1860	37.6	42.7	44.8	48.4	51.7	62.4	65.1	64.0	63.6	54.7	46.5	43.4	52.2
1861	38.0	43.4	45.4	48.1	53.5	56.9	58.4	59.9	63.3	52.2	*44.5	38.9	32.3
1862	24.1	31.9	41.1	47.0	56.9	62.7	64.3	55.7	58.1	50.8	41.4	39.3	48.5
1863	40.1	52.1	44.1	49.3	56.2	62.3	67.6	64.4	61.1	49.8	43.1	43.2	51.5
1864	39.4	44.5	43.1	50.6	61.0	61.4	65.3	65.1	58.8	50.2	44.3	36.8	51.8
1865	37.0	36.7	40.0	47.0	57.9	61.4	65.6	*64.4	*36.0	51.8	48.2	33.8	50.2
1866	36.7	36.0	45.1	48.2	*55.6	*60.9	*54.3	*64.4	50.3	58.2	47.7	48.2	51.1
1867	40.5	39.2	36.3	46.6	57.3	61.4	*54.4	64.3	56.8	56.2	46.7	40.0	50.6
1868	36.8	41.4	44.0										
Means	37.8	39.8	42.9	48.7	55.6	60.0	64.3	64.4	59.0	51.8	44.4	39.9	50.7

SPOKANE FALLS, WASH.

Year	Jan.	Feb.	Mar.	Apr.	May	June.	July.	Aug.	Sept.	Oct.	Nov.	Dec.	Annual.
1881	*23.2	29.5	41.4	45.9	53.1	59.3	65.0	61.9	53.5	42.9	33.0	31.3	45.5
1882	22.6	26.1	36.5	44.4	51.6	64.7	60.2	64.8	54.0	44.4	33.8	33.9	46.5
1883	23.8	18.8	46.6	46.0	55.3	65.3	71.2	55.8	57.7	44.3	39.0	29.5	46.6
1884	24.4	21.3	35.9	60.2	59.8	65.7	65.7	69.6	62.5	46.9	37.7	16.5	45.4
1885	21.9	36.6	45.7	56.8	57.2	63.9	71.3	70.0	59.6	46.0	41.1	34.8	50.1
1886	22.4	37.5	49.6	47.0	56.8	64.7	72.5	66.5	57.6	47.0	37.4	48.1	46.8
1887	31.6	18.5	43.6	47.0	56.5	60.2	78.0	66.1	56.7	45.6	36.7	22.0	47.2
1888	15.5	34.3	36.4	51.5	59.8								
Means	23.2	28.5	40.2	48.3	56.6	63.4	69.8	66.0	56.7	45.6	36.7	30.4	47.2

FORT SPOKANE, WASH.

Year	Jan.	Feb.	Mar.	Apr.	May	June.	July.	Aug.	Sept.	Oct.	Nov.	Dec.	Annual.
1883	*23.7	*23.6	39.7	47.9	58.1	67.7	73.3	58.8	57.4	44.2	35.3	26.7	47.1
1884	22.4	16.1	34.6	49.6	60.1	64.2	59.3	72.7	52.5	48.8	*37.3	*30.8	46.7
1886	19.4	36.4	41.6	49.0	58.7	66.2	76.0	66.9	60.8	46.9	42.3	38.7	50.4
1887	20.3	18.2	42.3	48.4	55.4	62.0	70.8	60.5	57.5	46.0	33.0	31.9	47.3
Means	23.7	23.6	39.6	48.6	58.8	64.5	72.3	70.3	58.0	46.4	37.2	30.8	47.8

TATOOSH ISLAND LIGHT-HOUSE, WASH.

Year	Jan.	Feb.	Mar.	Apr.	May	June.	July.	Aug.	Sept.	Oct.	Nov.	Dec.	Annual.
1869	*46.6	*39.6	*46.8	50.4	54.5	56.0	59.9	58.0	55.7	54.1	49.6	46.4	51.1
1870	45.6	44.1	42.5	49.3	52.4	57.5	62.9	60.2	57.3	51.6	46.0	45.0	51.2
1871	44.3	43.2	44.9	48.6	53.1	56.1	58.9	57.4	55.0	51.8	46.4	36.9	49.8
1872	44.6												
1883										48.1	44.8	42.6	
1884	41.6	36.6	42.7	48.2	50.9	53.3	56.8	58.4	62.9	56.1	46.4	36.0	47.8
1885	41.2	44.9	47.6	47.3	51.2	54.3	56.8	55.8	60.6	51.4	48.1	45.1	50.1
1886	39.5	44.4	43.6	46.6	50.7	54.8	57.6	56.6	53.7	52.2	45.5	45.9	49.6
1887	42.9	34.3	43.9	45.6	40.6	52.3	58.9	54.7	52.6	49.8	45.9	42.8	47.4
1888	36.4	43.2	43.2	46.5	46.6								
Means	41.6	41.3	44.2	48.0	51.3	55.1	58.0	57.1	54.7	50.0	47.2	43.0	49.4

FORT TOWNSEND, WASH.

Year	Jan.	Feb.	Mar.	Apr.	May	June.	July.	Aug.	Sept.	Oct.	Nov.	Dec.	Annual.
1859	36.3	36.8	40.9	36.2	52.9	58.6							
1860	40.7	42.6										41.4	
1861	38.4	42.5	45.4	49.0	53.3								

*Interpolated.

Statement showing mean temperatures—Continued.

FORT TOWNSEND, WASH.—Continued.

Year.	Jan.	Feb.	Mar.	Apr.	May.	June.	July.	Aug.	Sept.	Oct.	Nov.	Dec.	Annual.
1867									45.7	47.9	a 45.6	a 39.6	
1868	a 39.6	a 40.8	*44.5	a 49.6	a 53.9	a 56.5	a 61.2	56.8					
1874								a 54.3	a 63.5	*59.0	a 42.9	a 40.1	
1875	a 30.0	a 41.3	a 40.4	a 56.8	a 52.0	a 57.4	a 66.1	a 63.7	a 61.2	*50.0	*44.4	*41.0	49.9
1876	*38.2	*40.4	a 40.6	*48.4	a 52.5	a 60.0	a 66.7	a 68.9	a 58.7	a 52.9	a 44.1	a 41.9	49.9
1877	a 41.6	a 43.5	a 47.6	50.3	51.8	57.5	61.4	62.0	56.7	59.2	45.6	44.0	51.2
1878	43.6	45.9	48.8	50.7	51.3	60.8	60.1	61.8	55.0	48.7	46.0	40.5	51.2
1879	38.0	40.6	45.7	47.8	51.6	58.0	59.7	60.8	56.3	48.6	43.7	38.0	48.9
1880	36.4	36.1	38.7	47.7	60.2	56.6	56.7	50.7	54.3	*50.9	39.2	38.0	47.2
1881	38.3	43.6	47.0	*48.4	54.1	57.3	60.0	59.5	*57.5	48.9	44.4	42.1	50.1
1882	39.8	36.6	41.8	48.7	65.1	50.6	61.5	60.9	57.0	54.9	42.8	43.0	48.6
1883	36.0	35.8	48.6	47.6	58.4	59.2	62.7	60.9	58.0	48.8	43.9	42.1	48.7
1884	40.0	34.9	43.0	52.0	56.1	61.1	61.4	63.2	53.9	49.8	47.8	83.6	49.6
1885	40.6	47.0	50.7	51.8	56.6	60.3	65.3	63.0	56.8	52.5	*44.4	48.3	53.0
1886	37.7	15.4	43.8	60.2	55.5	60.4	63.2	62.8	57.4	49.5	44.0	44.7	51.2
1887	41.2	31.7	46.8	47.9	54.9	58.7	81.6	61.1	66.3	50.2	44.8	42.6	49.7
Means	38.2	40.4	44.5	48.4	53.6	58.8	61.7	61.4	57.5	50.0	44.4	41.0	50.0

UNION RIDGE, WASH.

1871							58.1	68.6	60.8	61.1	45.2	27.2	
1872	33.9	43.0	48.1	47.5	57.2	68.9							
Means	33.9	43.0	48.1	47.5	57.2	63.0	58.1	68.6	60.8	61.1	45.2	27.2	51.9

FORT VANCOUVER, WASH.

1849												34.8	
1850	38.1	41.0	37.3	56.8	56.2	81.8	67.4	66.6	61.6	63.8	48.1	35.8	51.9
1851	42.0	42.9	45.8									36.9	
1852	37.6	42.2	40.7	48.1	50.8	57.1	*66.1	*66.5	*58.2	68.9	45.1	38.2	52.0
1853	37.6	42.1	46.8	54.2	60.0	81.1	70.8	64.0	60.3	53.5	43.4	41.8	53.3
1854	*36.9	38.0	45.9	62.4	67.2	56.8	67.9	66.0	60.6	52.0	52.5	36.6	51.8
1855	42.1	43.7	50.9	51.5	57.6	85.0	*87.6	67.7	61.8	56.8	42.1	28.3	52.8
1856	27.8	43.8	50.8	51.1	60.9	61.6	66.1	64.2	62.6	51.5	43.4	37.6	52.5
1857	34.5	43.4	46.0	56.8	60.1	64.7	*87.6	67.0	61.2	53.7	45.2	42.2	53.6
1858	30.4	39.0	45.7	50.8	56.0	65.4	66.8	67.0	62.6	49.4	46.8	37.4	52.3
1859	37.2	39.5	41.8	50.3	56.4	55.5	87.3	65.4	60.9	53.6	30.8	31.3	50.7
1860	37.7	43.3	47.0	50.2	56.0	62.6	86.4	70.4	62.9	54.6	45.8	30.6	53.0
1861	30.9	48.1	47.8	51.2	53.7	60.4	67.9	66.3	52.5	61.5	48.6	46.1	52.3
1862	21.9	38.7	41.8	49.2	56.9	53.8	85.1	67.4	56.7	51.9	42.2	40.0	48.9
1863	40.8	39.4	48.4	51.4	50.0	64.6	72.2	66.1	63.1	50.2	44.0	42.5	53.3
1864	39.5	44.5	46.1	53.9	62.3	69.6	67.8	67.5	50.2	52.1	48.9	36.0	53.1
1865	36.4	37.5	41.2	49.0	60.2	64.8	68.5	58.3	*58.2	53.9	47.8	33.3	51.8
1866	38.1	37.0	47.3	51.4	*58.4	*83.2	*87.4	66.7	62.1	54.2	46.8	42.2	52.9
1867	40.8	41.1	38.1	53.5	61.9	84.3	64.3	58.1	56.8	49.6	44.8	40.7	51.8
1868	22.4	35.4	43.6	61.4	55.3	66.6	66.6						
Means	36.9	40.3	44.8	51.8	58.4	63.2	67.4	66.7	61.1	52.8	44.9	37.4	52.1

WALLA WALLA, WASH.

1869											43.3	37.2	
1874	34.8												
1877	*82.0	46.7	51.8	57.5	62.6	69.6	76.8	71.8	61.6	50.9	45.2	35.7	55.0
1878	36.8	45.7	52.8	54.8	61.9		71.4	71.9	50.6				
1879									63.6	49.7	37.9		
1885												41.2	
1886	26.8	43.2	44.5	52.0	61.4	68.0	78.7	73.9	64.0	50.2	39.8	39.7	53.3
1887	41.0	22.0	49.6	51.5	60.9	83.9	78.5	72.2	61.2	51.9	40.8	38.9	52.6
1888	22.1	45.4	44.7	55.1	64.8								
Means	32.9	46.4	48.6	54.8	62.3	67.2	75.0	72.4	62.0	50.7	41.2	38.7	53.8

FORT WALLA WALLA, WASH.

1857	27.4	38.8	46.6	*52.4	*63.3	73.0	70.9	75.8	65.7	55.8	38.6	38.6	54.0
1858	34.0	33.9	42.8	60.8	82.9	71.8	76.0	74.0	66.9	51.4	42.7	30.5	53.0
1859	34.7	34.7	43.4	51.6	61.1	70.4	80.3	74.8	65.8	61.8	34.6	27.4	53.8
1860	31.4	39.4	42.0	50.6	58.0	69.6	78.7	78.7	66.9	56.5	45.4	33.0	54.2
1861	32.1	44.3	47.1	58.1	86.3	85.2	78.0	74.8	60.0	51.8	42.9	38.3	54.6
1862	16.4	22.3	*42.5	47.7	60.9	68.1	*77.0	73.4	61.4	55.3	36.8	34.0	49.6
1863	38.1	38.8	*42.6	56.9	62.8	71.6	78.5	72.3	65.1	49.5	42.9	38.8	54.8
1864	35.2	44.8	46.2	56.6	88.5	67.2	77.7	75.4	64.2	52.7	42.3	31.4	55.3
1865	28.1	82.6	30.2	52.6	67.3	69.2	76.9	*75.0	*85.2	56.4	40.0	*22.9	53.7
1866													55.7

*Interpolated.   a Observations at Fort Townsend, latitude 48° 67', longitude 122° 44'.

CLIMATE OF OREGON AND WASHINGTON TERRITORY.

Statement showing mean temperatures—Continued.

FORT WALLA WALLA, WASH.—Continued.

Year.	Jan.	Feb.	Mar.	Apr.	May.	June.	July.	Aug.	Sept.	Oct.	Nov.	Dec.	Annual.
1907	35.0	39.2	33.6	53.5	61.6								
1875									66.5	60.6	38.7	44.3	
1876	26.6	45.2	48.7	51.4	56.3	71.9	76.2	70.9	66.6	56.9	42.6	29.4	63.7
1877	34.5	41.9	47.1	52.9	57.9	67.0	76.6	76.2	62.6	52.3	44.8	36.4	54.2
1878	37.7	45.5	52.9		62.0		78.3	77.8					
1879	30.6	38.1											
1896	32.4	37.9	46.5	54.2	64.2	70.7	78.7	76.5	66.2	52.2	48.4	40.4	55.6
1897	41.5	24.1	48.6	52.7	58.7	65.6	64.7	73.2	62.1	51.6	39.6	38.7	53.5
Means	32.4	27.8	44.3	52.5	61.8	70.6	77.6	75.9	63.2	54.6	41.6	35.1	54.6

HELENA, MONT.

Year.	Jan.	Feb.	Mar.	Apr.	May.	June.	July.	Aug.	Sept.	Oct.	Nov.	Dec.	Annual.
1860				36.8	48.3	58.7	60.7	63.7	56.7	46.2	19.3	9.6	
1861	9.8	25.8	30.4	47.6	55.4	61.4	58.3	66.1	54.6	37.9	26.8	30.8	43.6
1862	20.6	24.4	31.1	40.5	50.4	60.7	66.8	71.4	66.1	41.7	30.9	27.3	43.8
1863	18.5	14.1	34.2	60.4	49.6	61.8	66.7	87.9	58.8	38.3	32.4	27.8	42.7
1864	11.6	14.6	29.1	41.6	53.9	62.9	62.5	66.8	49.7	47.8	36.4	7.6	40.2
1865	21.0	28.2	49.6	45.7	51.0	56.8	64.7	64.1	55.4	47.5	39.1	31.1	45.4
1866	16.1	34.5	28.1	42.9	54.9	61.1	69.9	68.1	52.9	43.3	29.4	37.1	43.6
1887	20.6	5.6	40.3	42.4	51.5	57.6	66.0	63.6	56.6	42.9	33.9	22.0	41.9
1888	6.3	36.6	23.2	46.8	56.1								
Means	14.6	22.7	33.4	43.6	51.7	60.1	66.8	60.4	55.5	43.1	31.3	22.6	42.6

Appendix No. 6.

Table showing the temperature variability.

WASHINGTON TERRITORY.

Stations.	March. Mean daily variability.	March. 0° to 5°	March. 6° to 10°	April. Mean daily variability.	April. 0° to 5°	April. 6° to 10°	October. Mean daily variability.	October. 0° to 5°	October. 6° to 10°	November. Mean daily variability.	November. 0° to 5°	November. 6° to 10°	December. Mean daily variability.	December. 0° to 5°	December. 6° to 10°
Bainbridge Island (Port Blakely)	1.1	31	0	1.1	30	0	1.2	31	0	1.3	30	0	1.0	31	0
Colville, Fort	0.9	31	0	1.1	30	0	1.1	31	0	0.9	30	0	1.3	30	1
Cape Disappointment	0.8	31	0	0.6	30	0	0.6	31	0	0.8	30	0	0.7	31	0
Neah Bay	1.4	31	0	1.1	30	0	1.5	31	0	1.9	30	0	1.7	31	0
Olympia	1.0	31	0	0.8	30	0	0.9	31	0	0.9	30	0	1.4	31	0
San Juan Island	0.8	31	0	0.8	30	0	1.2	30	1	1.0	30	0	1.1	31	0
Stellacoom, Fort	1.1	30	1	1.1	30	0	1.2	31	0	1.4	30	0	1.3	31	0
Townsend, Fort	0.5	31	0	0.7	30	0	0.7	31	0	0.8	30	0	0.8	31	0
Vancouver, Fort	0.9	31	0	1.2	30	0	0.8	31	0	1.0	30	0	1.2	31	0
Walla Walla, Fort	1.4	31	0	1.3	30	0	1.3	30	1	1.9	30	0	1.8	31	0

OREGON.

Stations.	February. Mean daily variability.	February. 0° to 5°	February. 6° to 10°	March. Mean daily variability.	March. 0° to 5°	March. 6° to 10°	October. Mean daily variability.	October. 0° to 5°	October. 6° to 10°	November. Mean daily variability.	November. 0° to 5°	November. 6° to 10°	December. Mean daily variability.	December. 0° to 5°	December. 6° to 10°
Albany	1.2	28	0	1.2	31	0	1.1	31	0	1.0	30	0	1.8	31	0
Bandon	2.0	28	0	1.5	31	0	1.4	31	0	1.9	30	0	2.0	30	1
Camp Warner	1.9	28	0	2.2	28	3	2.0	31	0	2.1	29	1	1.0	31	0
Camp Harvey	1.5	28	0	1.2	31	0	1.1	31	0	1.0	30	0	0.8	31	0
Dalles, Fort	1.8	28	0	1.1	31	0	1.5	31	0	1.3	30	0	1.5	30	1
Kola	3.0	28	0	1.0	31	0	1.0	31	0	1.0	30	0	1.2	31	0
Hoskins, Fort	1.2	28	0	1.4	31	0	1.7	79	2	1.6	30	0	2.3	29	2
Klamath, Fort	0.7	28	0	1.0	31	0	1.4	29	2	0.9	30	0	1.3	31	0
Portland	0.7	28	0	0.7	31	0	0.7	31	0	1.1	30	0	1.0	31	0
Roseburgh	1.1	28	0	1.1	31	0	1.2	31	0	1.2	30	0	1.3	31	0
Stevens, Fort	0.8	28	0	0.5	31	0	0.7	31	0	0.7	30	0	1.0	31	0
Yamhill, Fort	1.1	28	0	1.4	31	0	1.1	31	0	1.7	30	0	1.6	31	0

IDAHO.

	February. Mean daily variability.	February. 0° to 5°	February. 6° to 10°	March. Mean daily variability.	March. 0° to 5°	March. 6° to 10°	October. Mean daily variability.	October. 0° to 5°	October. 6° to 10°	November. Mean daily variability.	November. 0° to 5°	November. 6° to 10°	December. Mean daily variability.	December. 0° to 5°	December. 6° to 10°
Boisé City	1.3	28	0	1.2	31	0	1.5	31	0	1.1	30	0	1.4	31	0

MONTANA.

	February. Mean daily variability.	February. 0° to 5°	February. 6° to 10°	March. Mean daily variability.	March. 0° to 5°	March. 6° to 10°	October. Mean daily variability.	October. 0° to 5°	October. 6° to 10°	November. Mean daily variability.	November. 0° to 5°	November. 6° to 10°	December. Mean daily variability.	December. 0° to 5°	December. 6° to 10°
Helena	1.6	28	0	1.2	31	0	1.4	31	0	2.1	30	0	1.5	30	1

Mean Annual Rainfall.

(in inches)

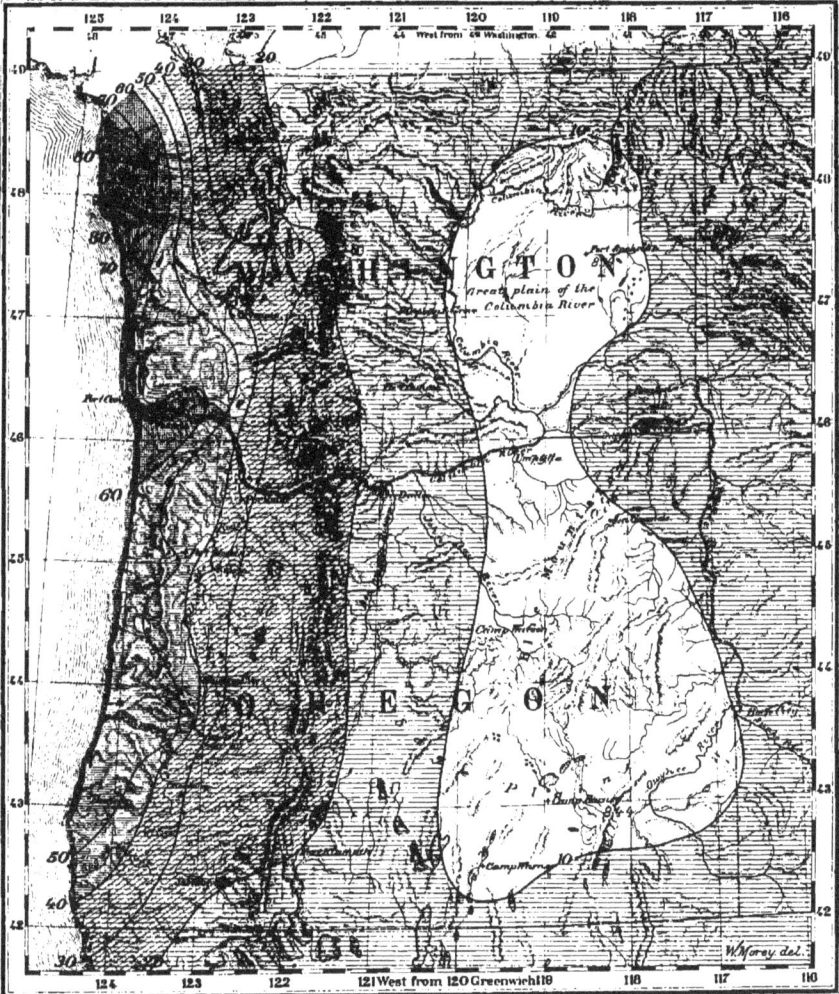

W. Morey, del. Sig Off.

Scale

100   50   25   0   50   100   400 STAT. MILES

PHOTO LITH BY A HOEN & CO BALTIMORE MD

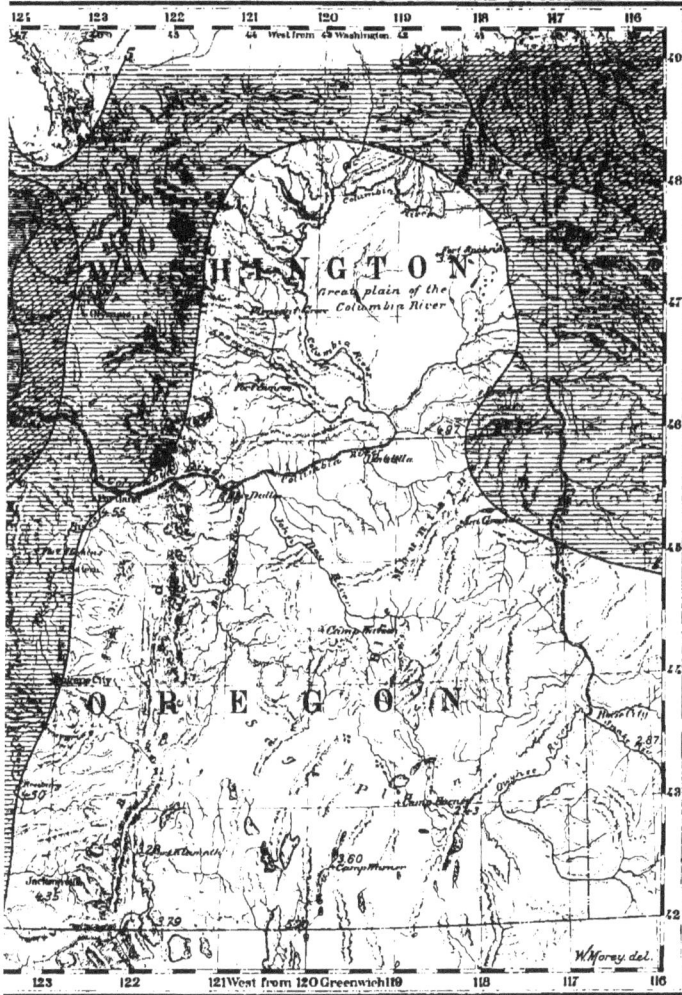

Mean Seasonal Rainfall.

(in inches.) *May - September.*

WASHINGTON

Great plain of the
Columbia River

OREGON

W.M.foray. del.

Average number of Rainy Days.

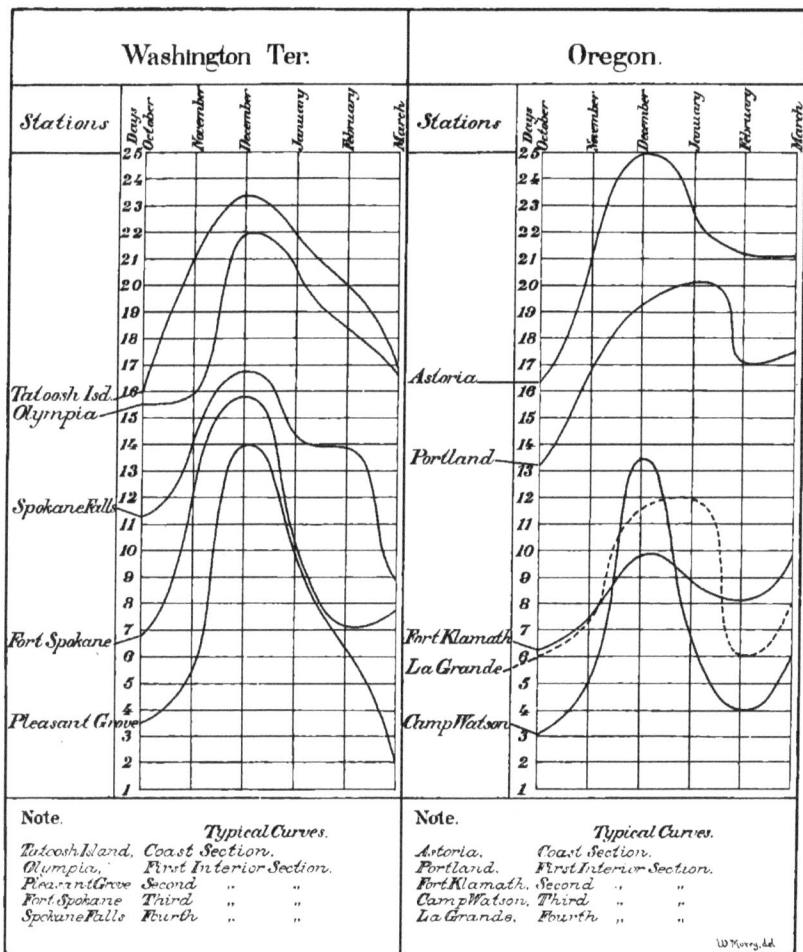

Washington Ter.		Oregon.	

Washington Ter.

Stations (Days October, November, December, January, February, March)

Tatoosh Isd.
Olympia
SpokaneFalls
Fort Spokane
Pleasant Grove

Scale: 1–25

Oregon.

Stations (Days October, November, December, January, February, March)

Astoria
Portland
Fort Klamath
La Grande
Camp Watson

Scale: 1–25

Note.

Typical Curves.

Tatoosh Island, Coast Section.
Olympia, First Interior Section.
Pleasant Grove Second „ „
Fort Spokane Third „ „
Spokane Falls Fourth „ „

Note.

Typical Curves.

Astoria. Coast Section.
Portland. First Interior Section.
Fort Klamath. Second „ „
Camp Watson. Third „ „
La Grande. Fourth „ „

W. Morey, del.

Mean Annual Temperature.

(in degrees Fahrenheit)

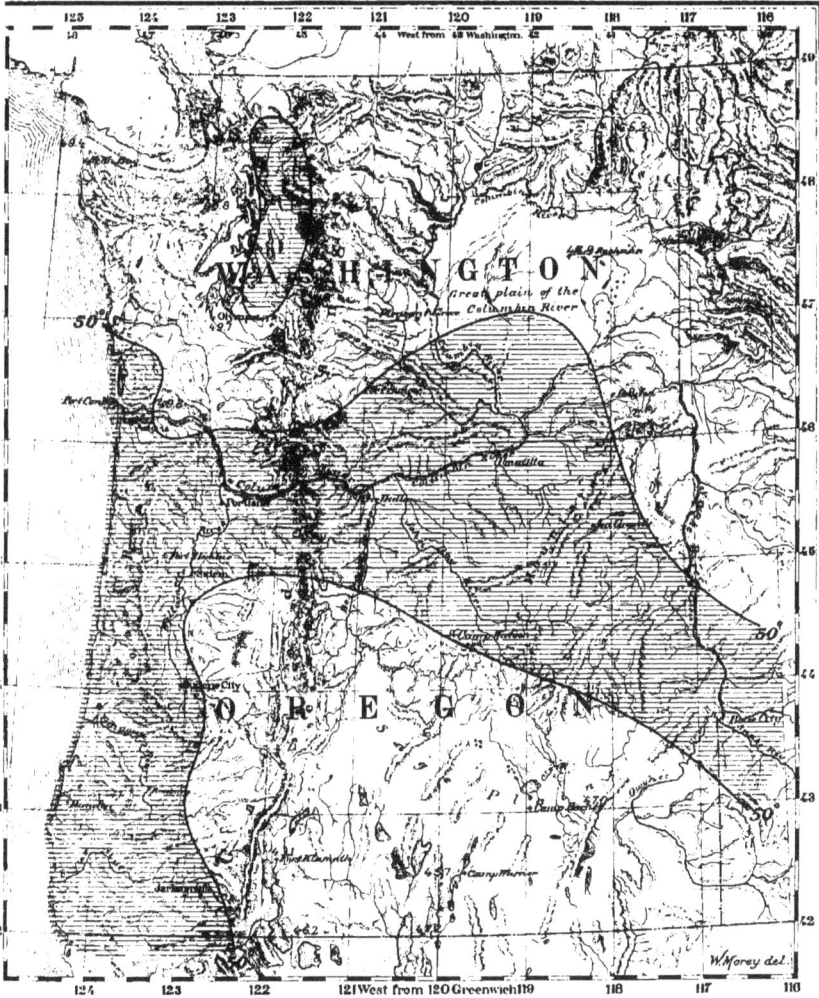

Mean Temperature.
(in degrees Fahrenheit.)

Summer.   *June–August.*

Scale

W.Morey, del. Sig. Off.

Mean Temperature.

(in degrees Fahrenheit)

W.Morey, del. Sig.Off.

Scale

100   50   25   0   50   100

www.ingramcontent.com/pod-product-compliance
Lightning Source LLC
Chambersburg PA
CBHW031815090426
42739CB00008B/1277